THE
RESTLESS
BELIEVERS

THE
RESTLESS
BELIEVERS

by

John J. Kirvan, C.S.P.

DEUS BOOKS
PAULIST PRESS
(Paulist Fathers)
Paramus, New Jersey

NIHIL OBSTAT: Rev. James J. O'Connor
    Censor Librorum

IMPRIMATUR: ✝ Leo A. Pursley, D.D.
    Bishop of Fort Wayne-South Bend

October 8, 1966

Cover Design: Claude Ponsot

Library of Congress
Catalog Card Number: 66-29818

Published by Paulist Press
Editorial Office: 304 W. 58th St., N. Y., N. Y. 10019
Business Office: Paramus, New Jersey 07652

Manufactured in the
United States of America
by Our Sunday Visitor Press

Contents

Introduction

The Restless Believers is a feeling book. It is closer to being a shared experience than a theological analysis. It records the experience of a man who allowed himself to "get involved," to be drawn into the problems of a troubled and turbulent generation of young Catholics. Some readers may think it lacks a detached perspective. They may find themselves wanting to know what all this implies about the Church and the individuals involved. They may want more detailed answers about what the troubled believers or their counsellors can do about the situation.

Father Kirvan by no means ignores these areas, but he has written a book with a different emphasis. The most important thing about this book is the seriousness with which he has approached the troubled believers and their problems. He doesn't just write about problems; he experiences them with the reader. His book is the record of what happened in the mind and heart of one thoughtful Christian confronted with the pain and anguish of other Christians. Father Kirvan doesn't juxtapose someone's preconceived answers (theological or otherwise) with the problems of another kind of human being called "students." He doesn't write from Olympus about "them." He enters into the seeking and searching experiences of the people he writes about. The primary strength and power of his book comes from the mutual concern and respect it communicates.

I am confident that the restless believers who read the book will recognize themselves and their problems (seeing them clearly perhaps for the first time) and will feel themselves to be understood and respected. Those who read it to help the restless will find that its openness and involvement is their own best guide.

During my years as a Catholic chaplain at Wayne State University, I shared with Father Kirvan many of the experiences and discussions that lie behind these pages. The substance of the book began to form in his mind during the four years he spent as a seminary professor. (Seminaries are institutions where, to the surprise of many, the restless believers already exist in great numbers.) But it was at Wayne State, among the honest, tough-minded students we found there, that its final shape took place. I am proud to recognize many of our late-night discussions in these pages, and proud also to have had a hand in writing parts of a few chapters. But most of all I am grateful to Father Kirvan for disciplining himself to write a book in the midst of the manifold and demanding duties of a priest who is both a chaplain to a large state university and on the staff of its Newman Center. My gratitude, however, is just the beginning, I am sure, of what he will hear in the years ahead from the restless believers and their counsellors who are lucky enough to read *and* experience *The Restless Believers*.

JOSEPH L. WALSH, C.S.P.
Chaplain to the Catholic Students
Brandeis University

1 Things Being What They Are

H<small>E WAS</small> eighteen, a freshman in college and for the last five minutes you shuffled through pleasantries to put him at ease.

Or she was thirty-five, a mother of three children, and for the last hour your conversation had picked its way through a dozen slight religious probings.

Or he was an old friend and drinking companion who suddenly at the beginning of the evening caught you off guard.

Or a hundred others in a hundred other ways.

With naked simplicity or in a fog of words they had said the same thing.

"I don't think I believe anymore."

These words spoken with hurt and/or confusion and/or defiance and/or pleading are heard too often these days to be startling. Most often it is a youngster who speaks them, but you can hear them from the lips of Catholic men and women two and three times as old.

Wherever and whenever men have believed, they have also doubted. It comes with being a man, with growth, with change. It comes because faith is a delicate and vulnerable thing. It comes because radically faith is a thing of God's generosity and impossible to unaided man.

Yet there is the feeling that the "crisis" may be wider and deeper in our own time than in other ages. The scale of the problem, however, is not the point.

The crisis exists for many. This is the point, the only point. And many are concerned.

America, the Jesuit weekly, has expressed its distress about the phenomenon of doubt among the young and described it as "new at least in its extent and openness."

In 1964, Brother Luke Salm, chairman of Manhattan College's theology department spoke to the society of Catholic College Teachers of Sacred Doctrine.

". . . The new generation of Christians," he told them, "is not at all prepared or willing to accept the doctrines of faith in the way that we or their parents were. The rising incidence of apostasy from the faith among the student population of Catholic colleges is not yet a matter of common knowledge."

That same summer, John Mahoney, a professor of English at University of Detroit was telling readers of *Thought* that the question was more one of quality than quantity.

"It is about the excellent student," he wrote, "or the exceptionally bright one, that concern must be raised, and about his own intellectual and religious future . . . Marriage problems, laziness, or what you will, may make other Catholics lapse, if they seldom apostacize, but these matters will not much bother the student we have been discussing. Like Stephen Dedalus, or the articulation of him which James Joyce gave, he will not reject doctrine, but its inapplicability. He may in a true and literal sense, lapse."

Others hastened to agree.

Theologian Eugene Burke of the Paulist Fathers drew upon two decades of teaching theology at Catholic University of America and Trinity College in Washington.

"I suspect," he said, "that there are more students with problems than we can count. In a Catholic college it is very seldom that they are going to tell you this is the case, but I would say that particularly in the last five years there is an increasingly articulate percentage who come up and tell you that they are not at all sure that they believe what you are teaching and that they are not at all sure that they have faith in any true religious sense."

Is this something new? Fr. Burke thinks so.

". . . That would never have occurred, I think, in a normal, ordinary Catholic college until five or six years ago. I think the fact was there, but to express it, to state it bluntly to you, this is quite new in my experience, and I think it may be only the top of the iceberg."

Sister Helen James John, also of Trinity College, recalled a meeting "at which students objected to the assumption that we are all committed Catholics."

Michael Novak, the articulate and accepted spokes-man for what he has called "the new generation" thinks that the figures on apostasy are extremely high, especially among the most creative. "In New York or Washington," he says, "it's appalling to see the ex-Catholics who are editors or junior executives. Professional circles are filled with these people."

"The real crisis in American Catholicism," he claims, "is not a crisis between aggiornamento and backwardness; it is a crisis between belief and unbelief . . . their real issue is whether this preposterous Church be divine."

Novak like the other commentators and educators is most concerned in his remarks with the young. But they are not alone.

A thirty-five-year-old husband, father, high-school history teacher knows the same kind of difficulties.

His central problem poured out in two long letters focuses on the Mass. He finds there little more than "a record of Western civilization, *old* Western civilization." He wonders whether he should stay away and hurt his family or continue with what he thinks is hypocrisy. "I do," he writes, "sincerely want to do God's will in my life. My greatest problem is that I'm no longer confident that taking part in a fossilized ritual of a vanished culture is doing God's will. Perhaps my real problem is continuing to accept the Church as a teacher — and the continued coerced attendance at Mass is only the irritant which forces my greater problem to the surface."

Another morning the mail is opened and in it is a letter from a fifty-five-year-old businessman, for many years a daily communicant, a man who finds time to teach CCD, work with a program of spiritual formation for college students, and who reads widely and well.

"I'm bothered," he says, "by all the evils in the world, and it's almost impossible for me to see a rational, just or loving God allowing this evil. The argument that evil is the result of original sin seems to me to be the worst kind of sophistry. Can you imagine using this argument on a bunch of Jews about to be gassed? Or that this earns a place in heaven, or is for the greater honor and glory of God, or is a punishment for past sins — each one is full of holes." He has the feeling that so many thin answers have been given by religion that today even what is sound becomes suspect.

"I don't think," he adds, "my problem rests so much in believing in God as it does in believing in the supernatural powers of the Church. Although even my faith in God is weak; it's almost an agnosticism. Although I'm left with the conclusion that there is 'Something' out there, the leap from that to a personal God is almost impossible for me."

Both of these men, neither one a college youngster facing first questions, are afraid that they will lapse. They won't specifically reject the doctrines. They will, simply, in John Mahoney's phrase "conclude to its irrelevance." As the younger of the two says, "I'm a believer and not likely to stop being one." The older man confesses: "I do want Christ to at least let me know he's there. I do want to believe in Christ."

Both men have come to a turning point.

The businessman puts it this way. "How I would like to go back to the past. None of these things ever

5

entered my mind. It would be simple for me to lead the Mass-on-Sunday, keep-the-sixth-commandment type of religion. But that's not true. I couldn't go back, not now. If that's all there is to Catholicism, it's a sham."

These men are far from alone in their problems. Thousands of others share them. These men, perhaps, are more sensitive, feel the questions more sharply, can articulate their problems more clearly.

What is beyond question is that at this turning point these men look for help.

They seek more help than comes from a piously remembered: "A thousand difficulties don't make a doubt." A thousand difficulties can swallow a man. So can a dozen. So can just one — if it's the right one.

He doesn't need to hear: "Forget all this intellectual nonsense . . . Go home and say a prayer . . . It's your pride . . . Look at all the great minds who have been good, humble Catholics."

What he needs is more difficult to say. But some things are certain.

He needs to know that questioning isn't a death warrant for faith. It can be the birth of a new, deeper, more mature commitment. Indeed, he must know that the faith of a child won't serve a grown man, and that the transition is a kind of death. Like any death it has its pain and anguish.

He needs to know that in every believer there are strains of unbelief. That every man who can begin a prayer: "I believe," must be prepared to end it: "help my unbelief."

He must know that faith goes beyond accepting a creed intellectually. It involves him as a total person.

And tangled in his assent are psychological fibers, as well as educational, historical, family and social ones.

He needs to be able to sort out what is truly of faith, from an inheritance of pious addenda and childish simplifications. He may need to discover that what he questions and rejects are only caricatures.

But what he most needs to know is another believer who is an honest and reflective man. He needs to encounter true belief and not a charade.

Sister Jacqueline Grennan, president of Webster College puts it this way.

". . . They will have to find you not only approachable but extraordinarily empathetic. They have to believe that for you also religion cannot be all cut and dried. They have to see this in you. This means that you have to admit to yourself and then let them see that you too go through periods of terrible darkness and terrible unknowing."

And she adds this hope.

". . . Were they to meet a sufficient number of open Catholics they might feel again that there was room, even for them, within the Church."

None of this means, of course, that every Catholic youngster between the ages of fifteen and twenty-one is currently running around in a stage of crisis.

Many young people wouldn't even know what is being talked about, either because family, educational, and emotional background have made it easy for them to move from one stage of faith to another, or because out of reflex or fear they have managed to bury most of the difficulties that have occurred to them.

For many others, religion at this period of life

is simply not demanding enough to bring them satisfaction, or cause them any sleepless nights. They feel no need to think about or make decisions about religious questions. Still others keep it out of the foreground of their thoughts until some decision is actually required, which in this country seems to coincide with marriage. It's not unusual to find young people who have been in church only rarely for several years suddenly insisting that they be married in church. Religion, it seems, for many is part of the package marked "settling down."

For many youngsters, therefore, religious difficulties at this stage of life are not profound enough to cause real worry for anyone concerned with their welfare. They'll find their way back to religious practice. What kind of religion they'll return to is another question. It may be every bit as shallow as that of the childhood which in every other respect they have left behind. And this should be a matter of concern.

Generally it will be true that without some kind of "crisis," without some turning point in the life of faith, it will probably not grow into the mature commitment that is the mark of religious adulthood.

However painful such crises may be, they are not generally to be prevented or escaped from. Through them can come a deeper, livelier, more relevant religious life. Without them there is seldom any substantial growth.

For a teacher or counsellor to try to induce such crises, however, seems the height of irresponsibility and is every bit as foolish and dangerous as avoiding them when they arise naturally.

A crisis of faith is not something to be played with. It's much too painful and too potentially destructive for anyone to go looking for. Anyone who raises questions for a believer must be prepared to help in the search for answers.

Chances are, however, with today's young generation of believers that there won't be much call for raising questions which the youngsters haven't already raised.

The responsibility is to know and understand the context in which the questions are raised, the origin of the questions, the reasons for questioning at all, and some insight into the significance of the questions.

In all of this some advice once given by Frank Sheed is very important. Questioners are to be answered, not questions.

Faith is not a series of definitive answers to neatly phrased questions. Faith is a total human being responding to the person of God. When faith is in trouble, a whole person is having trouble with a relationship, and not just with one or two formulas. A crisis of faith is a personal crisis. The questions which are raised may be only a focus point for problems that are much deeper.

Those problems can be of a psychological variety that are present in all times and places, or may be problems raised by the here and now. They may focus on God, on the Church, on the impact of pluralism, on the lure of the secular.

The Restless Believers

But whatever the questions, for whatever reason they are raised, they must find their ultimate answer in the discovery of the faith of Abraham as it is possible and fruitful for this individual, unique person, at this moment of his life.

2 All Times, All Places

OF ALL the problems connected with the crisis of faith not the least is the phrase itself.

The word *crisis* is a hang-up.

There's no question that it's a melodramatic word that produces instant visions of creased brows, teary eyes, gnashing teeth and wrung hands. For the spiritually well-read it invokes John-of-the-Cross-size dark nights of the soul.

Maybe this is because it's a word with a medical history, where it has come to describe that moment in the progress of a disease which indicates whether the result is to be recovery or death.

Actually it merely refers to that point of time when it is decided whether something is to go on, be modified or terminated. A turning point. A decisive moment.

If it were not so cumbersome we would probably be better off referring to *turning-points-of-faith*. It carries less emotional baggage. It says what has to be said. And it takes the experience out of the realm of the exotic and sets it down in the pedestrian day-by-day world where it really belongs, usually occurs and is best encountered.

Crises of faith are simply those times in a man's life when, consciously or unconsciously, easily or painfully, by acting or by failing to act, a man decides to go on believing, modifies his faith or ends it.

If this still sounds dramatic, look at it this way.

A growing child suddenly discovers he has lost interest in games and toys that have entertained him for years. He turns to things more in keeping with his age group. The carefree bachelor decides it's time to settle down. The young man finds middle-age advancing and slows his pace.

These are crises, turning points. But they are expected parts of growth, part of what it means to be a human being. Even those who fight them are not too deeply surprised by them.

The same sort of thing happens on the level of faith. A child's faith, like his toys, gives way to the demands of adolescence and a changing vision of what is real and important. And in turn the adolescent's faith gives way to that of a man.

To see the crisis this way is to expect it, and to be spared, amid a dozen other shocks, the shock of surprise or the guilt of feeling that something must have gone wrong, that God must be displeased.

The young man or woman sits across the desk from a priest or speaks from behind the grill of the confessional: "Gee, Father, I don't know what's gone wrong. But I just don't believe like I used to. When I was in grade school and for the first couple of years of high school I was real religious, and now I just don't seem to care."

The youngster feels sick at heart. He feels deeply guilty. Yet the chances are that the only thing wrong with him is that he's growing up. He suffers from being a human being subject to change.

This isn't to gloss over the pain that is almost inevitable. Nor is it to water down the dangers of the experience or its riskiness. It's simply to state a fact of our humanity that will challenge some and petrify others.

The youngster is passing from one stage of his life to another. There is a kind of death involved in the transition, for one level must die if the other is to be born healthy. Usually there's no clear moment of death. There is a kind of over-lap, one stage of life slowly losing its grip while another begins a slow rise to dominance.

The over-lap causes its own confusion and pain. The new man makes his appearance with a new set of values, self-fulfillment, independence and freedom. But the old man lingers with standards of judgment of what is right and what is wrong, obedience, respect for elders, blind faith. The youngster knows the demand of his new visions and feels their validity, but he feels condemned by the standards of his old world.

The crisis of faith is more often than not a crisis of development.

Let's take a closer look at one of these crises — the development of the child into the young man or woman.*

* Here we are greatly dependent on Guardini, Babin and Godin as anyone who has read their work knows well.

The Restless Believers

The faith of a child like the rest of his world has several characteristics which make radical change not only inevitable but necessary, but also leave it particularly vulnerable to loss with the passage from childhood.

For one thing, a child doesn't draw clear distinctions. In his world dream and reality are all mixed up together. He doesn't really care about distinctions between work and play, symbol and object, fact and fancy. Heaven and earth are pretty much the same thing. So are bible stories and fairy tales. So is God and man. Divine and human reality are mixed in together. Of neither is he critical.

The divine realities which are the object of faith are always clothed in human words and images. The process begins in childhood where the image and the reality are, for the child, not distinguishable. When for example, a child is taught to think of God as our Father in heaven, what the child really does is think of his own father. He may make him bigger than life size, but it's still his own father. Heaven is a playground or a big house filled with fairy-tale creatures called angels. And the love of that "heavenly Father" is only as real as the embrace of the father he knows. Something wrong here? No. But it's important to know that these are the terms in which faith begins, because someday those images will shatter, the clay feet will be visible, the experience open to questions.

Faith, by the same token, is always tied up with the faith of others. We go to God through men. There are persons in the lives of each of us whose faith provided the incentive for our own. There are people from whom we derive our convictions and with whose

14

support we maintain them. There are relationships in which our faith takes its shape. There are friends and teachers. But above all, especially for the child, there is the mother and father. None of these relationships remain the same over the years, and some of them disappear. Faith can't but be affected by the changes.

The most important thing to know about the faith of a child, however, is that the faith he possesses is not really his *own* faith. He has the faith of his parents, his teachers, his friends, the people who surround and mold his life. His faith as a conscious thing is really environmental. It belongs to the structure of his life. But someday he must make it his own.

Before that day comes, however, the youngster will have passed through at least two separate periods of his life, the ones we lump under the catch-all called adolescence. At each point his needs will be somewhat different, and so will be his religious attitudes. At each point he will be further invited to make his faith personal. But at the same points he will feel the temptation to abandon the same faith.

In the first stage, the one Babin calls Pre-Adolescence (11 to 14) the thrust is to break through the closed world of childhood. The world outside the family appears and appeals as strongly as it will ever again in a man's life. And the youngster begins to strain toward that world of which he so much wants to become a part. He conforms to it. He copies it. It's a period of doubt and suspicion in which the youngster vacillates between longing backward glances at the security he has known and compulsive ventures into the world of playmates, sports heroes, movies and forbidden books.

From his adventures the child may reap a harvest of first personal convictions, but he may also come to know scrupulosity. But mostly he will experience estrangement from his parents and their values (including religion), loneliness and self-pity. It's a negative or, at best, neutral period marked by "freedom, separation and destruction."

In the second period, what Babin calls Pubescent Adolescence (14-16) the mood is far more positive. There's lots of energy, but it goes off in different directions. Emotions are intense and the young believer becomes intensely aware of himself. The whole world, in fact, gets shaped and judged in terms of his own personal need for fulfillment. He accepts those standards and beliefs which conform to common sense and the good impulses of his own heart. In his "I"-centeredness there is often no room for God, at least that God who makes himself present too concretely, in institutions, dogmas and authorities. But there is at the same time a real sense of the sacred, as the young man meets it in sunsets, remote and dark corners of the church, in ceremony and excitement. Naturalism is the key and, often enough, sentimentality the dominant pitch. It's a time of enormous enthusiasm and high idealism. Out of it could come the full-hearted believer, but so could there emerge a man disillusioned at the disparity of his "pure" ideals with the humanity-tainted Church.

Both of these periods are only stepping stones, however, to what Babin calls Late Adolescence (16-20), the period in which the ground is directly laid for a fundamental religious choice. For if the final choice is

16

not yet possible, it is at least being compounded from a whole series of decisions and commitments which together fix the basic direction of the young believer. In these decisions there are two other levels of experience at work. For even as the decisions are being made, the young man is aware of both a deep insecurity and a deepening intellectual possibility. The insecurity arises with the knowledge that early adolescence with all its turmoils and doubts has left him with no solid structure or direction to his life. Confidence-shaking questions arise: Who am I? Where am I going? What am I going to do with my life? But this new insecurity, unlike that of the earlier years in which emotions ran wild to victimize him, has a new serenity about it. It comes from being for the first time in a position to reflect upon himself with his deepening intellectual capacity. He is now conscious of the need to put some order into his life. He feels the need for fundamental choices.

This is the normal cycle in which the crisis of faith evolves. For faith is not exempt from the laws of human growth.

Out of the struggle of these years some will emerge with a strong and mature faith. Those who do probably made it through the shoals for a variety of reasons and people. During those years they met both understanding authority and needed freedom. They met teachers who demonstrated that they knew and appreciated the problems. They found a community of believers with whom they could give of themselves to their highest ideals. Instead of reprimand and condemnation they were faced within religion by opportunities that challenged them to use their new freedom responsibly. And

17

above all they inherited an image of God as someone who loved them.

Others will emerge as non-believers. It would be easy to say of them that it's their own fault, that pride and selfishness, a closed mind and a sin-hardened heart took their faith away. But the judgment may be far from right. For some will have arrived at the periods of crisis with an image of God that no man could long live with, and found no one or no thing that could introduce them to the God who brings hope and meaning to life. For such persons the signs through which God makes himself present and approachable may have been so distorted by experience that they could no longer speak to the reality of their deepest human needs.

But there are still others who refuse not only the temptation of unbelief but the invitation to mature belief. These are the youngsters who are petrified by the responsibilities of maturity and who can never or will never make the passage from one stage of growth to another. Too often they try to hold on to their childhood faith and their childhood world. Some try to sleep through the evolution of faith. Some pretend the questions will go away if they just ignore them. Some believe that the only real faith is the faith of childhood and treat the invitation to a different kind of faith as a temptation to sin. Some have been told that to question is to sin. But most are just afraid.

But whatever the eventual outcome of the adolescent years, two things must be kept in mind.

The first is that belief in God and love of parents are the only two basic things which a child somehow tries to bring through all the passing phases of his life.

There is no one who does not know how difficult it is to try to remain faithful to one's family as he struggles for an independent, self-fulfilling life. The struggle to remain a believer is every bit as hard. Everything else of childhood — games, friends, neighborhood, values, school and opinions — can be left behind with a minimum of pain. But God and parents, the Church and the family have got to be brought along, transformed and renewed but somehow intact. It can be enormously difficult, guilt-filled and agonizing.

The other thing that must be kept in mind is that the crisis of faith is a completely normal and healthy experience. Its broad lines will probably be those which we have sketched above. But for each individual it will be an unique experience. It will be made easier or more difficult by a whole variety of factors: the health of the family life in which it occurs, the solidity of the religious education which precedes it, the temperament of the believer, the sympathy of teachers and friends, the community in which it is experienced, the precise moment in history when it occurs. And a dozen others. The basic point is that no youngster should be told that God is displeased with him because he has these difficulties. He must not be frightened into trying to abandon his own growth. He can't do it. The forces of development are too strong and too real. He must not be led to think that belief is incompatible with his humanity.

To experience turning points, crises of faith, happens to all men. We have concentrated on the turning point that young people know. But it's not the last they will experience. As the enthusiasm of their young

19

adult life wanes and they come to know that many of their dreams will never be fulfilled, they will know crisis again. And when old age approaches, so too does another turning point in the life of faith.

It happens at every juncture of a man's life, in all times and all places.

3 Here and Now

Put twenty people in a room who all profess the same Catholic faith and if you dig even an inch beneath the catechism answers to your questions you'll find twenty different ways of believing the same things.

No two believers are alike. Not even if they share the same teachers, the same pastors and read the same books. Not even if they share the same parents.

The objects, the raw material of faith may be the same: the existence of God, the Trinity, the divinity and humanity of Christ, the sacraments. But faith isn't a pill to be swallowed or even a contract that needs only a signature to be valid.

At its deepest, faith is a meeting with God in Jesus Christ and through the Church. It's a person-to-person affair. And the response of the believer can no more be defined by formulas than Jesus Christ can be summed up in those same formulas. No two people know a common friend in exactly the same way.

21

Between two brothers the differences may be subtle.

But between generations you can expect the differences to be great.

There are, of course, the psychological factors which make it unrealistic to expect the same faith in a ten-year-old as in a forty-year-old.

But there are other things at work seeing to it that a faith shaped in 1966 is going to be different from one that came to maturity in 1930. There are powerful historical and social forces.

The act of faith is always made at a given historical moment by a man who in ways that are sometimes crude, at other times subtle, is a product of his time. God may be beyond history but believers never are.

History is that mixture of politics, economics, culture, education, social structures and religion which define the days in which a man lives. And during which he believes or doesn't.

History can move a man toward or away from faith by providing reasons for both.

It can and does frame the questions which a believer must confront, and with which he confronts God. It shapes the form in which faith expresses itself. In short it sets a scene to which not just faith as an act, but its language, its gestures, its way of behaving must be relevant or must fail.

This means that the eighteen-year-old of the 60's comes to a religious turning point with motives and questions shaped by his times. It means that if religion does not speak to him in language and gestures understood by his history-shaped generation, it may never be heard. It means that whatever faith emerges will express itself in ways different from men who have been shaped by other moments of history.

Let's make it concrete. Let's look at the youngster who is today facing a turning point in his faith.

The eighteen- to twenty-one-year-old believer of today was born in the second half of the 40's, and the years of his life have been marked by events large enough to affect anyone's approach to God.

He and "the bomb" entered the scene at about the same time. Adults may pooh-pooh the effect of this experience, but probe the mind and memory of a twenty-year-old and you'll find scars. "I used to have nightmares," remembers a young girl. "I would wake up my parents with cries of 'the bombs are coming.'" The same girl and a current friend of hers both remember being routed out of class every day by practice air-raid alarms, and being taught how to throw themselves on the floor of a concrete-walled cellar. The brother of one of the girls used to ask his mother: "Will they still be fighting when I grow up?" A college science major admits that when a jet goes over at night he looks out to check for telltale colors in the sky. "The bomb," says another, "is inevitable and impossible. What it does is make all my hopes and plans meaningless." Still another, with the same pin-point accuracy puts it this way: "Why plan for the future? There isn't going to be any."

The "bomb" would be enough to make this generation different, but it's far from alone as a shaping force.

This generation has never been protected by distance. It's not just that destruction can now be delivered around the world with increasing accuracy. It's that "a small world isn't it" has blossomed from cocktail-party cliché into pressing reality. Within minutes a struggle in Asia is known in Atlanta. The world is at their doorstep, and the time has long since passed when a child is confronted only by the problems of his own neighborhood. He can watch a foreign war, "live and in color" every night at 6:30. For years he has fallen asleep and awakened in a home invaded by all mankind.

Technology is thrusting this generation into an age of cybernetics, a computerized society. As they prepare for marriage and responsibility they wonder about the world into which their children will grow. They wonder how long before a machine replaces them. Their very humanity seems threatened by the inventiveness of their own genius.

They know, by experience, that knowledge is accumulating so rapidly that it becomes obsolete before it is absorbed. As a result, moral decisions which in the past could rest on a fairly stable body of knowledge find themselves in a context of expansion which requires that many decisions be on a level of discovery. There is little by way of time, place or agency for the synthesis of what is learned. Inventions multiply without evaluation of their effect on the mankind they are destined to serve. And absolutes become unthinkable.

And by way of a final turn of the knife — as the world shrinks its institutions get bigger. This is the age of "the big." Big business, big labor, big government, big education threaten to reduce the individual to a code number. A New York clergyman feels compelled to tell the graduates of a posh school they must ponder: "How can we survive in a world in which the only way to be noticed is if your I.B.M. card gets bent?" But the young believer who attempts to turn to religion to find personal meaning often encounters more bigness — a big Church, big dioceses and big parishes. How can he feel important?

All of these factors, together with others, are at work influencing the young Catholic as he attempts to make a lifetime religious commitment. For them is emerging what Philip Scharper with apt metaphor calls "a new mankind." This new man, unchanged as he may be in his essential human characteristics, "grasps himself, understands himself in a way that is markedly different from the self-awareness and self-understanding of man even at the beginning of our own century."

What is this "new man" like?

For one thing he is a man almost obsessed with *personalism*. A Catholic college graduate summed it up this way for an NBC Catholic Hour audience: "My generation is rampantly personalistic. The whole bit is personal. We're looking for, I think, a personal commitment, something we can really involve ourselves in individually." He goes on to claim that his generation is not interested in "the ultimate causes of philosophy . . . but in the more contemporary existential concerns: What am I? Who am I? Where am I going? What's really meaningful?" He wants to know what it means to be an authentic human being, what it means really to be a person.

But this personalism doesn't drive the new man into isolation. At the same time that he is concerned with personal fulfillment, he is intensely aware of his need of

25

others. "Community" is a sacred word, even though when pressed to define it he may end up stuttering about "I-Thou relationships." He knows what it isn't: a blind bureaucratic institution in which people don't know or care about each other. He suspects that structures are its enemy. And so he looks for small almost intimate groups where the spirit of community can be experienced in a way not possible in huge institutions. The experience of community — a shared experience of unity, respect and mutual acceptance — has become the purpose and value of life.

The problems that concern him are "people" problems. He has no strong sense of loyalty to institutions. He may consider things like patriotism "phony." His government and its symbols are part of the establishment, things taken for granted and not the sort of thing that arouses his emotions. There is little pride, for example, in the Church as a far-flung institution that has weathered the storms of history. Much less is there any loyalty to his parish, or school. These are part of the structured, given (soon to be automated?) aspects of life. He looks elsewhere for spirit and life.

Where he looks is where people are suffering from institutions and the insensitivity of others. He goes to Alabama and Mississippi. But not precisely to register voters and provide education. He goes more to express his solidarity with other persons who are suffering, and to protest what is wrong and rotten in society. He is not a classical reformer but a human being trying to express deep, personal human feelings. If social advances emerge, that's fine. But the big thing is being *there*, not just *here*.

Not every eighteen-year-old is going to think this way of course. Large numbers are not going to think of anything except the diploma which acts as a passport to a job. The lives of others revolve around "beer and babes."

But those who are thinking this way bring these same values, needs and attitudes to their confrontation with religion.

Bluntly, this means that religion must offer an opportunity for personal fulfillment, a deep sense of personal importance, an experience of community, and a relevance to the social problems which concern the young. If it doesn't they will look elsewhere. For the reality of these needs is far more pressing than a childhood faith which growth alone has already brought into question.

It means the young man is not going to ask questions for which answers have been neatly prepared in the armory of traditional apologetics. And when he is provided with them he will not so much argue against them as be indifferent to them. He may not understand them, but if he does he may dismiss them as irrelevant.

It means that certain aspects of the Church such as its history, size, power, accomplishments and tradition instead of impressing him may repel him as just so many more examples of the things he feels called upon to reject.

It may mean that the very core of Catholic Christianity, the sacramental encounters with Christ may be lost on him. And here we are at the very heart of the problem. Charles Davis in one of his many single-page masterpieces for *America* puts it sharply:

"The visible Church is still designed for men of a different culture, and it has not yet adapted itself to the greatly changed sensibility of modern men. Feature after feature clashes with present affectivity. The feelings it arouses often confuse, bewilder and mislead, unless transposed by a fine historical sense."

Davis uses the sacraments as an example. They are meant to be moments in which a man experiences the unity of the spiritual and the material. Faith tells him he is about to encounter Christ. But he is to enjoy this experience in a human structure, an event that he knows through his senses. They are to provide, as Davis says, "an affective experience of our faith, enabling us to apprehend its realities with an assent that engages our imagination and emotions — in fact all that we are as bodily persons."

But it doesn't happen for many, particularly the young. For them the faith with its sacramental encounters is meaningless. The problem isn't fundamentally intellectual. It's that the forms in which faith is enveloped belong to another age, and do not speak to them today.

Instead of helping them to faith, the forms often hinder. "Instead of beginning," says Davis, "with an affective experience through which they can pass to the realities of faith, they have to begin with an unsupported, spiritual faith and use this sheerly spiritual faith to give some meaning to what they are asked to do. The strain is too much for those whose faith still has to grow."

There is still one more difficulty to be faced by any new generation of believers.

It is the question of *models* in the faith. What is it like to be a committed Catholic? For the answer he must look to his fellow believers. And here the age gap becomes crucial. He may respect and admire his parents and their generation for what they have achieved. But he may in the same breath reject their way of life. They had their own problems and they solved them in their own way, and from their solution emerged a style of faith which may have nothing to do with the real issues of the new day. At least as the youngster judges it.

This misunderstanding may be as inevitable as the age gap itself, but it makes it even more difficult for the young Catholic to make a mature decision to remain a believer. The devotional life, the societies of his parents and their apparent acceptance of evils that hurt him, seem to define the Church. After all they are Catholics, firm and committed over many years. Perhaps to be a *real* Catholic you have to be like them. And so he begins to wonder whether there is any place for him in their Church.

One thing is certain. A new generation of believers will not and cannot accept faith as a heritage. They won't accept it as part of some family tradition. They cannot accept it as some manifest destiny. Either it is something in which they can find needed dimensions of their own desperate search for self-identity, or they will abandon it as irrelevant.

One other thing is certain. Faith is a personal response, and young Catholics need to know that faith

29

is never twice exactly the same. It has a core which is true in all times and places. But with every new, maturely committed believer it is uniquely experienced and differently expressed.

4 Morals? Maybe?

It was at least fifteen years ago that some editor dashed off a clever reply to a reader who had written about students having intellectual difficulties with the Church.

But it was the kind of line you don't forget.

"Intellectual difficulties of students," he announced, "are only skin deep."

That settled everything of course. Everybody knows that when you talk about students, or even older people, there aren't any "intellectual" problems, there are only "moral" problems. And for *moral* read sex.

"No one," wrote another distinguished apologist, "loses his faith without first losing his morals."

Without question, it sometimes happens this way. Perhaps more often than not. But hardly ever with the simplicity promoted by the sloganeer moralists.

For one thing such simplifications have the not-too-subtle suggestion that unbelief and immorality are close to synonymous. They suggest that God operates

31

in human life primarily as a policeman of our be-
havior, and that without God most of us would go on
a rampage of sensuality.

Such thinking is bad at three points. Is displays un-
forgivable naïveté about the dimensions of modern
unbelief. It emasculates religion. And it ignores the
depths of human needs.

There are superficial, flippant, I-live-for-kicks-man,
gin-mill atheists. But there are also honest men who
don't believe, men with definite ideas of the good life,
men who are dedicated, moral, filled with purpose.
There are men who deny religion not because it limits
their sex life but because as they see it religion is too
easy, a way out of true human responsibility. We'll
come back to this later. But for the moment, it's
enough to say that the wise man will stop and think
before he jumps to the conclusion that every doubter
is a libertarian.

The easy equation of doubt with moral problems
also sells religion short. There's no question that a
belief in God acts as a powerful restrainer on human
passions. But a belief that never gets beyond a string of
taboos isn't worth much. A God who is no more than
a faceless lawgiver is going to be scrapped in any
normal human growth. Catholicism is not just an ethic;
it's a personal encounter with Christ in his Church.
If that encounter doesn't occur, a man may doubt
just as surely as when his morals fail.

It sells man short too. The sex drive is strong;
almost as strong as the drive to life itself. No one
denies that. But there are other forces in man. He has
a need to be honest with himself. He has a need to

understand. He has a need to love and feel loved. He has a need to be his own man, to become what he can be. He has a need to be free. And these are strong drives too — strong enough to make a man doubt when the God he has known (even if it be a caricature) or the religion he has practiced (however incompletely) seems to stand between himself and his humanity.

For at least these three reasons it's bad business to assume that a doubting man need only get control of himself.

But it's also bad business to pretend that in many youthful failures of faith moral problems don't play a major role, although not always in the simplistic pattern that is often assumed.

Take Tony for an example.

He was masturbating for two years before he found out that the Church taught that this was a mortal sin. He was an almost daily communicant who suddenly came to believe that for two years all his confessions has been bad and all his communions sacrilegious. And by this time he found it almost impossible to stop the practice he had begun without malice.

His high school years in a Catholic institution were hell. The priest teachers he faced in almost every class became for him constant reminders of the just God who was going to send him to hell. His classmates became strangers, alienated from him by his sense of sin. He was sure they all knew what he was doing and hated him for it. His confessions became a torture either because he met instant condemnation or because more often than not his guts would run out on him when he tried to tell the truth about himself as he saw it. On Sunday mornings he went to communion with his parents because he couldn't let them know he was in trouble.

When he finally got to college he had lost every bit of self-respect. He didn't date because he didn't expect anyone else to like him. By the end of the year God was gone. And Tony was at ease with himself for the first time in five years. His life was getting into perspective, and he felt free to develop the rest of his humanity. He had a set of values he could live with. The torturing God was dead.

With teachers better trained in modern catechetics, with the advice of confessors more adept in psychology, Tony might still be able to believe in God. But now he doubts.

At first Tony's doubts were a defense mechanism. Today they are deep and real. Six years ago Tony had a moral problem. Today it is faith. It won't help to tell him: "Go to confession and your problems will pass." If Tony will ever return to his faith it will have to be with the discovery of a God he has never before known, a God who will not strip him of his dignity.

There are thousands of other young Catholic males who have shared Tony's anguish and melancholy, who have known his inability to persevere in frustrating efforts to overcome a sexual habit. Some still live with the pain, but many others have followed Tony into disbelief.

Many others have found themselves in love with a partner whose moral standards were far different from theirs. Still others feel curiosity about pre-marital sex experience, the fears of gnawing tendencies to homosexuality, the social pressures of fraternity-sorority life. Young marrieds know the birth control dilemma. And most experience a natural period of boredom and indifference which accompanies the late teens and early twenties.

Father Robert Kavanaugh, campus pastor at Michigan State University, a man who has heard the questions first hand, lists the areas where the problem begins and then adds:

"It begins morally but gradually undermines the self-assurance of the believer. Doubt is the only way to lift the agonizing pressure of self-hatred that accompanies those who begin to be involved in these moral problems. Those who fail in the crisis could better be described as having lost their courage than having lost their faith."

Not all young people solve the conflict the same way. Faced with the turbulence of their adolescent years, they may agonize like Tony or they may, as so many others, separate religion and life into two airtight compartments. A Catholic college graduate from Boston told his interviewer on NBC's Catholic Hour: "I don't think the sexual difficulties Catholic students have are religious; they're moral." Theologians might wince at the vocabulary, but the meaning they would grasp. It's as if the graduate said: "Religion is one thing. The pressing facts of life are another. Religion has to do with God, and going to Mass on Sunday and not eating meat on Friday. It has nothing to do with the way I feel right now, the things I need, the fears I know, the hungers I experience. Sin is saying 'no' to God. I'm not saying 'no' to anybody. I'm saying 'yes' to what

I know is real and present. What I do on a date has nothing to do with the way I feel about God."

But whether the young man or woman goes through the anguish of trying to keep his life and faith together, or settles for the "two camp" approach, the result is often the same. At the end, loss of faith. At other levels the same thing happens. A young couple faces the birth-control question. A young couple break out of a marriage that was pure hell and are told that for the rest of their life they must be celibate. The heroic is beyond them. More in regret than in anger they are out of the Church.

Of all of them somebody is going to say: "They lost their morals, that's why they lost their faith."

Whatever else it is, it's not that simple.

What has happened is this. A man has faced, perhaps for the first time, a large moral-religious question. And in the confrontation the Church stands outside him like a faceless, inhuman machine cranking out ready, universal demands. What he feels inside himself seems real. What he can check and test seems real. What he judges he needs to be himself seems real. But the Church seems unreal.

Bluntly he tells you in the confessional or across the desk: "I don't really think any of these things are wrong. I don't believe they're wrong. The Church says they are. But that's not enough. I don't do things or not do them just because somebody tells me they're right or wrong. I have to see it for myself."

Write it off as intellectual pride or moral decadence if you want to. It'll make you feel better but it won't help the human being who is struggling for maturity.

For the truth is that believers are made or unmade
in these moments of crisis. And the further truth is
that in their youthful struggle with sex, most human
beings face the demands of Christianity for the first time
in a crucial way. You can go further. If Kinsey's statistics are even eighty percent true, then as Michael Novak
points out, most Catholic men form their fundamental
moral convictions in terms of a bout with masturbation.
And in that same context of moral choice they make a
fundamental decision about the relevance of religion
in general and of the Catholic Church in particular
to their lives.

The problem is made harder by the fact that the
moral choice is being made at the very moment when
a person is struggling through the pain and confusion
of moving from one level of ethics and morals to
another.

In childhood years our ethics are on what Louis
Monden calls the level of *instinct*. Our impulses are
dammed up by a wall of pressures, from parents, society and reality as a whole. We learn that there are
some things we ought to do. But that "ought" is felt
as something outside ourselves and in fact opposed to
ourselves. We sin when we transgress a taboo. And our
guilt is a blind feeling of having acted badly against
some order outside ourselves. Our sorrow is simply an
instinctive urge to avoid the consequences of what
we've done.

Some men, no matter how sophisticated other
dimensions of their life might become, carry this instinctive morality far into adult life. The adolescent

certainly has it when he faces his first big moral crises.

But at the same time he is trying to develop an ethic on what Monden calls the *moral* level. He means a morality that will spring from the conscious and free self-realization of the human person. The law here is the demand from within him that he move toward his own full and final self-development. This is his fundamental moral obligation. Sin is to act against that conscience. Sorrow is to know that he has freely gone against himself.

On still a higher level, the one Monden calls *Christian-religious,* a man finds his law in the offered love of Christ. And sin is to reject that love.

This highest level exists at least as a seed even in the child. But it doesn't prevent man from moving painfully and slowly from level to level. It's a matter of growth. There's law at work here, too.

The young man facing his first large moral and religious crisis is often caught between the first and second level of human moral growth. He has barely emerged from a period when morality was essentially obedience. He has only one unsure foot in the world of conscience and self-fulfillment. But he is intensely aware of the pressures from within demanding that he be himself, even as he moves with some sense of guilt from the world where right and wrong was what somebody else told him it was.

In every other department of his life he is making hesitant steps into the world of independence. But here at the very point where his humanity is its most demanding, he hears voices demanding obedience to laws he never thought of before and which he cannot understand even now. Obedience is not enough. But his conscience is still too unformed for him to have made his own the subtle laws of love which alone can govern his need for sexual satisfaction. He has been caught off guard. And the Church sounds like nothing else but a referee with a loud whistle.

At this moment his greatest strength or weakness will be his image of God. If he has been led toward a God who is a loving Father, he will have someone to turn to. And the pain of his failures will be assuaged by the forgiveness of the God he trusts and tries to love. But if within him he carries a picture of God as a policeman who waits around every corner to catch a man in the moment of sin, he will have no one he can trust. The God who alone can forgive him, who alone can make it possible for him to live with himself, is a God who is merely biding his time, waiting to damn him.

So it's true.

Loss of morals does often lead to loss of faith. But it's by a circuitous and painful route. And too often it's because the Christianity which should have given a man hope and courage has been so distorted within him that it becomes instead the very heart of fears and agony that are too much for any man to live with.

5 The One and the Many

REMEMBER this line from the course in apologetics? "The Catholic Church is the sole divinely authorized teacher of revelation."

For youngsters it's put more bluntly. "You belong to the one true Church."

The point here is not to challenge this description of Catholic Christianity but to point out the kind of demands it makes on a person making a decision about his future religious life.

This Catholic claim to uniqueness makes, it seems to the believer in crisis, demands that run exactly counter to the whole thrust of his education, the facts of his culture and to his personal needs at this stage of his growth.

His education makes him extremely suspicious of anyone who claims to have the whole story on anything. Either/or, black/white approaches he assigns to childhood and grade school. His teachers have been busy for years insisting that he be critical. They have pushed, pulled, coaxed and forced him into both/and, grayish judgments. Those who claim to have final, complete answers to any human problem are probably either fools or charlatans.

Science has been the touchstone. He has watched laws that his parents thought were unquestionable fall into irrelevance. A century ago men looked at the world as a closed system of laws that bound reality together in a tight, neat system of causes and effects. The picture has changed. Instead of necessity there are statistics which allow for all sorts of probabilities. Instead of determinism, there is indeterminism. This is the generation of the quantum theory that forbids a man to say anything final about his world.

One thing is certain from his education. "Tomorrow may bring a new answer." Today we go with what we've got. But don't close any doors. It's an open world.

It's also a big world. And a varied one with dozens of cultures, a multitude of ways of looking at things and doing things, a variety of values, a plurality of beliefs. It's a no-neighborhood world where no one can build a wall high enough or strong enough to keep out the flow of contradictory and complementary ideas. It's a pluralist world, one that goes beyond admitting many shades of conviction to insisting that many are better than one.

Many young Catholics feel the impact of pluralism and know its attractions. Most experience its challenge.

42

Johnny's mediaeval ancestor lived in a closed society where faith and citizenship were part of the same package and objects of the same pride and loyalty. His American ancestors found themselves as strangers in a new land. Their religion with its common heritage and friendships gave them security and identity and a loyalty that grew under seige. But Johnny has grown up with playmates of a dozen beliefs, and has been educated in schools that are committed to none.

Johnny knows, in a way that his ancestors did not, that his Church is part of history, that there are other forces and institutions which are calling the shots, and forming all the brave new worlds, and that none of them have exclusive rights to mankind's needs.

His own needs seem to run counter to the Church's exclusive claims. From his earliest days he has been told that his religion is the one true one, the correct one, God's religion, in a way that sets it apart from all others. But that's just the rub! Like other bright, intelligent, well-behaved young Catholics he has been submitted to years of systematic exploration of his faith. From the age of six to the crucial, late-teen turning points he has been part of a Catholic school or some other fairly well organized program of religious instruction. Now he's being told: "Commit yourself. Make this Church your own. Accept it as the one true Church." And he replies: "This is the only one I know. How do I know if it's the one, the true. Or even just better. Until you know what else is around, how can you choose this one?"

He puts a premium on honesty, on authenticity.

43

And he has a feeling that to continue to believe in the Church of his parents is the easy, thoughtless, inexpensive thing to do. Even more cutting: he feels trapped.

A nineteen-year-old puts it this way:

"How can I possibly make a real, honest decision either for or against staying in the Church. I'm in it aren't I? And you tell me it's wrong to look around. That it's a sin to suspend my judgment and check the other possibilities seriously, not just out of academic curiosity. If I don't know what's it like to be a Protestant or Buddhist or an atheist, how can I ever really choose to be a Catholic?"

Through the years when faith and nature are both demanding that the young believer make a mature choice, he is also being asked to continue to make an unqualified commitment to the uniqueness of Catholicism.

Most of the time he will do it, but often enough on the grounds that he'll go to hell if he doesn't. He does it out of resentment. He does it with a deep sense of the fact that — "I don't really know if I believe this, but I've got to or else my life is going to be all fouled up."

When a student comes to the seeking, questioning period of his life, Catholicism doesn't appear to be something new and exciting in which he might discover answers to his deepest questions. On the contrary it's part of the baggage he has carried with him through childhood, puberty and adolescence, and which is now as much a problem as it is a problem solver. It's one more thing to be questioned, and not the sort of thing to which he wants readily to respond: "This and nothing else."

So what does he do?

For one thing he may attempt to blur the edges of his religious identity. Ask him what he is and instead of saying "Catholic" he may say "Christian." Not everyone who uses the broader label does it for the same reason, but there are many younger believers who would agree with the young Catholic who said: "When you say you're a Christian you get rid of the whole hierarchical structure, and you wash away all the things which you see as wrong. You get right down to basic Christian beliefs — charity and faith, motivation and commitment — without ever getting involved in the structure itself."

And if you call yourself a Catholic?

"It means that you are going to be answerable for almost everything that's gone on, or is going on. And I don't know as I'd be willing to take that on. If you say you're a Catholic to some people, right away you're in for a good fight. They're going to throw at you everything from the Inquisition backwards and right up to today. Sure they're wrong, but it happens. If you say you're a Christian then there aren't many people who will argue with you."

Part of the same package will be attempts to avoid making the inherited commitment any deeper than necessary. He's going to sidestep efforts to make him say more than he believes and to act with more conviction than he has. But it won't be easy. At this point there will be all sorts of efforts from parents, teachers and chaplains to get a sign of commitment from him.

"You should make a retreat . . . Join the men's club
. . . Get involved in an action group . . . Be a com-
mentator at Mass . . . Join the Newman Club." All he
may be capable of or willing to do is keep up his Sunday
Mass attendance, Friday abstinence, and an occasional
use of the sacraments. He can't "honestly" do more.

He may, of course, want to experiment a little and
to make an occasional, token, declaration of independence. So once in a while he skips Sunday Mass and
orders a hamburger on Friday. He may know better
than anyone else that they are feeble even childish
gestures, and that skipping Mass on Sunday out of
defiance is every bit as stupid as attending Mass out of
fear. But it's not defiance that he has in mind. It's just
to prove to himself that he can do it, that he's still a
free man no matter how deeply enmeshed in faith his
family and school life have been.

Occasionally a bigger break will seem called for.
Instead of a haphazard gesture here or there, he begins
to think in terms of a deliberate program of freeing
himself from his roots. "I've decided," he tells a friend
or counsellor, "to stop being a Catholic at least for a
while. I'm going to suspend all my judgments and start
all over with a completely clean slate. From this
moment on, I don't believe anything, I don't accept
anything. Maybe I'll end up as a Catholic, but it's going
to be a free choice." It's impossible and it's phony, but
for the youngster who feels driven to become his own
man it all seems reasonable. He doesn't know yet and
has to discover that no one can disinherit himself, that
he's got eighteen or so years of history inside him and
the brush hasn't been made yet that can wipe a human

slate clean. There's just no returning to Eden, childhood or an unshaped soul. He has to discover, too,
that the honesty he so treasures isn't helped by trying
to be somebody other than he is, that this artificial pose
can never be much more than an act. Honesty in faith,
and freedom in commitment, he'll have to discover, are
to be found in his own depths plumbed and not in roles
played.

He may, of course, do something that will throw all
his observers off balance. He may go to Selma or
Mississippi, or join in the work of an inner-city settle-
ment house, or tutor potential drop-outs, or work in a
hospital. He may become startlingly active in Christian
social action programs or show a sudden burst of enthusiasm for theology courses and liturgical experiences. He
may show all the signs of someone who has found his
commitment and is now making it practical. But the
opposite may be the truth. Instead of acting from commitment he may just be looking for it. What he has
done is picked out a problem that is real for him and
then put Christianity to the test. The problem is real,
but does Catholicism have anything to do with its
solution? He goes there looking for himself. And he
approaches classes and liturgy in the same way. Do
they have anything to say to him that is real? His faith
is at stake.

He does the same sort of thing quite informally
day in and day out by throwing tough questions and
outrageous positions at anyone who will listen and especially at his parents and religiously committed teachers.
He wants to see and hear their response. If they are
disturbed (which he hopes they won't be) he'll go away

justified in his doubts. More than answers, however, he is looking for signs of thoughtful conviction, sympathy and trust. What he fears most of all is that they will prove to be shallow and afraid, and that they will write him off either by not taking him as seriously as he has a right to expect, or by emotionally excommunicating him.

So what's to be done?

The first thing is not to miss the point.

The point is not precisely the *doctrine* of the Church as one and true. It's the *kind* of commitment that is implied. The believer isn't saying exactly: "I don't believe in one, true Church." Although some do say exactly this. Most, however, are in effect saying: "What does the doctrine mean in my life and my world?"

For this kind of problem, accumulations of historical, philosophical, scriptural and theological arguments are not the solution. A hard-headed review of apologetics won't do any harm and may illuminate the issue but for the most part it won't do much good at this point in the questioning.

What is necessary is that he be allowed to experience the Church as a commitment within which he can not only retain his freedom but enhance it. On the part of all concerned this is going to take patience, time and honesty.

One young Catholic spells out what he thinks is needed. He talks specifically of religion teachers but what he says applys to advisors and parents too.

"It's entirely up to the teacher," he says. "It's going to depend on how he approaches the subject, how he presents it. His approach can be and often is . . . it's closed, it's absolute . . . There are really no important questions to be asked . . . Everything's solved. . . . Trent said everything. The teacher can do this, but if he does he has lost the interest of the student who has just begun to question himself. The student doesn't want to begin by knowing all the answers and then finding questions to them; it should be the opposite. He should be allowed to develop his own answers. And if they are not parallel to the official pronunciation, then perhaps they should be allowed to develop toward the official answer instead of saying, 'No, that's not right.' "

"In many ways," he continues, "they don't want answers. They want direction. They want to find out for themselves. When a priest or teacher tells them 'No. No. That's all wrong. The doctrine is this. The dogma is this,' that priest has lost his audience. He's lost his chance; he's blown the whole bit."

This takes patience. It takes a man who really believes that no one can be cajoled or forced into commitments that are worth their salt. It takes someone who believes that a commitment to faith is not just some form of assurance against hell, but a positive dimension of a full human life. And that this kind of commitment takes time to flower.

It means not flying into panic the first time a youngster decides that he's going to skip Mass or raising a fracas at the first announcement: "I'm not sure I want to be a Catholic." It means taking the time to help the youngster frame his deepest questions and then helping him to search for his own answers. It means giving the youngster in the midst of his search an experience in his counsellor of the Church deeply concerned about the depth, the honesty, the authenticity of every man's belief.

It means trying to understand what it's like to suddenly discover that you can't just accept what others tell you, and what it's like to live in a world where a thousand possibilities are just opening. It means not underestimating the pull of the many, nor the seriousness of committing yourself to just one.

6 When God Dies

IN OUR town you can sport a garish, red-white-and-blue bumper sticker that proclaims "God is Alive."

It's somebody's bright idea for offsetting current rumors to the contrary. But it's doubtful if any new slogan is going to satisfy thousands who without ever reading a line of the radical new theologians feel deeply in themselves that "God *is* dead . . . absent . . . missing . . . unfelt . . . irrelevant."

The question before the house, then, is God. Not in abstract terms of whether he is or isn't, or what he's like or isn't like. But whether in the mid-twentieth century you can experience him.

The operative word, *experience,* is enough to give most Catholics digestive problems because they associate it with visions of revival tents and Billy Graham crusades. And that's not a very Catholic cup of tea.

It's certainly not one of those words, moreover, that became rote in catechism days. More's the pity because this is exactly what is at stake for many young Catholics who are having God problems.

When someone says: "I can't believe in God because he's so unreal," or "I can't seem to find God," or "The whole thing about God doesn't say anything to me anymore," he's probably saying "I haven't," or "I can't seem to experience him." This means, "I can't feel his presence."

Now there's always going to be somebody in the house to rise up in protest about "feelings." "After all," he says, "you can hardly make belief in God subject to ups and downs in your adrenaline supply." True. But hardly the point.

What is the point?

The point is that knowing God is completely different from knowing that two and two make four. God is not a mathematical sum, a logical conclusion, an historical deduction or a scientific hypothesis. If he's anything at all he's not something but someone. And to know him is not just to know that he is but to respond as a total person to him. It's not just believing *that* he is, it's believing *in* him. "Belief in" goes far beyond simply acknowledging that someone exists. It means even more than finding that person trustworthy. To believe in someone means that you're willing to put yourself in his hands. Let's say it — it means love.

At the heart of religion there must be an experience of God and the problem is that today people are finding that experience very hard to come by.

Where do you go for it? Where do you look?

There was no problem in childhood. You looked to your parents. You believed in them and so you believed them when they told you that there's a God up in heaven who takes special care of little boys and

52

girls. Perhaps, for good measure, they also mentioned that this God gets even with little boys and girls who cross streets when they are not supposed to and otherwise commit major childhood crimes.

But when parents are no longer infallible, and you have to make your own commitments, where do you look then?

The traditional place is the world, nature.

On its most basic level this turning to the world in search of God comes down to asking "Who made it?" You are presented with a staggering array of intricate unities, complex designs, laws of growth and orders of power and beauty. "How did all this come to be? Surely it wasn't an accident. Somebody did it. Somebody made it. God."

At this level God is an answer to questions.

For some God will always come as the answer, and the world will always be a sacramental place.

But for many others who search the face of creation, God is not the only, if any answer, and the world has lost its mysterious, its sacred quality.

A youngster raised with chemistry sets, and zoology kits for playthings and who builds rockets in the backyard is going to look at the world in a completely new way. For him there are going to be no more mysteries in the world of nature, just problems. He's not going to need God to fill in the gaps of his knowledge, just time, education and curiosity. He may well become one of those for whom, in Bishop Robinson's phrase: "God is intellectually superfluous."

This is a double-edged sword.

It cuts at the belief of the youngster who is making

his first foray into discovering God for himself. He's left without one of the hardiest of all helps toward the discovery of God. At the very moment when he needs reasons to believe in God he can't come up with the world as one of them.

But it also cuts, and even more deeply, at the faith of the youngster who has built his case for God around creation, and over a period of education discovers that his arguments won't hold up in the face of his new scientific attitudes. If he has leaned toward a "God of the gaps" (again, Robinson's phrase) with the closing of the gaps he may find himself not just without reasons for God's existence, but without God himself.

The fundamental problem, of course, is that when God appears primarily as an answer to questions about the universe, the best that can be expected is a belief *that* God is, and not a belief *in* him. And "belief that" cannot stand much more than token opposition.

It's a question, too, whether nature can ever yield more than answers to questions, whether it can ever lead a man to belief in God.

Religious people have traditionally said yes. The world for them is sacred. It comes from the hands of God and is marked with his fingerprints. It doesn't just point to God, it reveals him. The world is a place where you find God. It's a place where you meet him, encounter him, experience him. It's a sacrament in which through the external signs of his creation God speaks and man responds.

Bishop Robinson puts it this way.

"The man who finds himself compelled to acknowledge the reality of *God,* whatever he may call him or however he may image him, is the man who, through the mathematical regularities and through the functional values, is met by the same grace and the same claim that he recognizes in the I-Thou relation with another person."

He finds in the world not just problems to be solved or realities to be lived with, but a demand for a full-hearted personal response. He feels called upon to make a response of a kind not justified by the appearances of what he confronts. He feels the presence of Someone.

Responding to the demand is neither automatic nor easy. It makes demands. In this encounter the person is not permitted to stop with the simple acknowledgement of the presence. He cannot just *believe that* Someone is making a claim. The encounter is such that it demands *belief in* that someone. I-Thou relationships mean love, mean shifting the center of your whole being. They can and should shake a man to his core.

It's important, too, to realize that this encounter never takes place between some abstract man and some abstract universe. It takes place between a man with a personal history and the universe in a particular place and time.

The world yields only what man is prepared to see. It can speak to men only in whatever language they are prepared to understand. The alienated, isolated, intensely lonely man will perhaps find God in the world, but it may be a God who seems to reject him. The frightened man finds an angry face. The confused may be further confounded. A man takes in things according to his capacity to absorb them. His personal history filters the evidence.

Tennessee Williams makes this point sharply and deeply. In his play *Suddenly Last Summer,* he tells the story of a poet and his mother who went looking for "a clear image" of God. They journeyed to the Galapagos Islands in their search, and the poet, Sebastian, found what he was looking for in a spectacle of nature.

Once a year the great sea-turtles — the females — crawl up onto the beaches of these islands to lay their eggs. They deposit them in the sand and then crawl, half-dead, back to the sea. In due time the eggs hatch and the sand becomes black with the new-born turtles who as soon as they leave their shell make a run for the sea. In the same instant, however, the sky becomes black with great carniverous birds who swoop down on the turtles, flipping them over on their backs to expose the soft underside, which they rip, claw and devour.

The poet "spent the whole blazing equatorial day in the crow's nest of the schooner watching the scene on the beach of the Encatadas until it was too dark to see it, and when he came down the rigging he said, 'Well, now I've seen him' — and he meant God."

He could just as well have said: "Well now I've seen us, me, my mother, all men." For in the play the beach scene is used by the author to dramatize the relationship of the poet to his mother. Sebastian is looking for a personal relationship with God, and the only terms which he has to understand personal relationships are the ones he has already experienced.

In starker terms: belief in God is knowing that you

are loved by him, and returning that love. It's impossible just to be told that this is true. You have to experience it. This means that your capacity to believe in God is radically dependent on your own experience of human love. An adult who does not know what it is to love and be loved may miss the whole point of whatever experience of God he might have.

Sometimes, too, when a person opens himself up to an experience of God, he becomes unsure of himself. He is afraid the experience is only an illusion. "I want so much that there should be a God that I've talked myself into believing there is," he says. "Maybe the experience I have is just wish-fulfillment."

Such fear shouldn't surprise anyone. It's the natural fear that must rise in a man at that point where he must make the leap from knowledge to commitment. He has come to believe *that* God is, and now he must respond to that knowledge by believing *in* God.

This is a big step, and it will be possible only if he has had. If he is to enter into a personal relationship with the God he has somehow experienced, that God must be somehow personified. For the Christian this experience of God, this divine element in the world that makes a claim on him, is substantiated and personified in Jesus Christ. In Christ he recognizes in concrete, personal terms beyond the possibility of illusion the claim he has felt deep within himself. In Christ he discovers what he has felt called upon to believe in, what he has felt called upon to commit himself to. Christ verifies his experience, justifies his faith.

How a twentieth century man experiences Christ
is, of course, another question in itself.

The answer which is easiest to give is the Church
with its scripture, sacraments and liturgy. This is the
special place where man is promised a meeting with
Christ whenever and wherever he encounters it. Christ
himself made the promise and it's not about to be
challenged.

But it's also true that to tell a youngster — "Go to
Church, receive the sacraments and say your prayers"
— borders somewhat on the magical. He won't be able
to do without these things but a lot will depend on
where, when and in what circumstances he follows
the instructions.

A quick visit to a harried confessor, offering the
Mass in the supermarket conditions of a large suburban
parish or having the scriptures read to him in the
tones of a courtroom bailiff are not the best conditions in which to make a personal encounter with
Christ. He may, in time, be able to rise above the
conditions, but for the moment it's asking too much.

If he finds Christ anywhere it's most likely going to
be among his peers in small groups where Christian
values and the face of Christ become visible in a personal, demanding way. Wherever two or three are
gathered together in his name, Christ has promised to
be present. Multiply that number by three or four and
you have the situation in which youngsters today find
it easiest to respond to the claims of God in Christ.

It doesn't take much. Or many. Or perhaps more
than one occasion.

It may be a small intimate celebration of the

eucharist by a group in which all present know each other by their first names. In these moments the young believer can almost physically sense the Christian values of brotherhood and unity. He gets a glimpse of the love of Christ, of brotherhood under one Father.

Or it may be in a social action or discussion group in which he begins to know that he is not alone in the vision that he has caught, however tenuously. He begins to realize that the values he has caught sight of are real and powerful, and the faith which has begun in him is no will-o'-the-wisp but something with meaning today.

Wherever and whenever it happens, one thing is certain. He won't be able to do it alone any more than he could as a child. He will have to find himself in new communities of believers whom he knows and trusts and with whom he can share his questionings and doubts and new-found experiences.

He will need these reassurances to cover the pain that comes when the God of childhood dies, to be replaced with a deeper, more personal, more demanding God of his mature years.

For many it will only be in these experiences of the Church, of its scriptures, its sacraments and its liturgy that he will find verification in Christ of his experience of God.

7 Institutions? Who Needs Them?

I<small>N AN</small> upstate New York Catholic high school they surveyed the students and discovered that substantial numbers no longer believe in God or prayer. But the real kicker was the discovery that a larger percentage of these Catholic young people don't believe in institutional religion.

Translated into more pedestrian terms that reads: Religion may be OK, but Churches are out.

There are several pretty shallow reasons for taking a position like this, but there are some good ones too.

"Institution" and "Christianity" seem to be contradictory terms to some youngsters. You can't have one if you've got the other. Religion is a personal thing. Not especially in the subjective sense that "it all centers in me." Not even in the sense of "God and my soul." But in the sense that it's a person-to-person thing, something between my neighbor and me and God. It's love. Institutions, on the other hand, seem anything but personal. Too often they appear to be faceless, mechanical bureaucracies. According to one student: "You don't have to join a club to love your neighbor or God. Love is a person-to-person thing, a moment-to-moment thing that has its roots in spontaneity. When you organize something like this it dies."

"Institutions tend to exist for their own self perpetuation," said another student, a college senior. "The energies that should be spent on religion — such as making God visible and real, the service of people and true worship — get sidetracked into keeping the club operating. All the energy, time and personnel that should be used for preaching the Gospel are spent financing, administering and maintaining the organization."

Many young believers feel that the official representatives of an institution become more interested in the needs of the organization than in the needs of the people the organization was formed to serve. They tend to feel that the man with the Roman collar, when presented with problems, settles them on the basis of what is good for the organization rather than what is good for the individual person. Bishops, priests, nuns and brothers wear the uniform of the organization, and young people are tempted to wonder whether their answers would be the same if they had less personally at stake.

The difficulty becomes less subtle when the charge is phrased this way: "It seems to me that the Church becomes a substitute for God. I get the impression that it's more important that I should be a card-carrying parishioner, than that I should love God and my neighbor."

The same objection to the Church as an institution gets another kind of phrasing. "Institutions lose their freedom. When you've got parish plants to support, churches, rectories, schools, convents, hospitals and what have you, you've got to think twice and maybe three times before you say something that might offend one of your sources of money. Sometimes it seems the Church is so in need of support for these programs, even if they're worthy, that it can't afford to preach the whole Gospel."

Institutions, some young believers feel, are also essentially divisive. Religion which should have the goal of reuniting all men in a common brotherhood settles down instead into separate camps with everybody protecting his own flank. Instead of reuniting men, new, highly volatile divisions are set up.

But closest, perhaps, to the heart of a young believer in the mid-twentieth century is a deep-rooted suspicion about all institutions. On them he blames the conflicts of our time, and he has come to believe that you can expect nothing but betrayal and dishonesty from them. They are the great instruments which have worked to reduce men to ciphers. They are the prophets of depersonalization. They are something that religion should stand against. But when religion is institutional it has surrendered to the very forces which are its deepest enemies.

Now that's some bag of complaints.

The most troubling thing for young believers in these attitudes is the paradox they express. Young people themselves are aware of it. The paradox is this: highly developed institutions like the Church or the federal government seem to stifle personal initiative by their very organization; ways of doing things are long ingrained; the "method" becomes sacrosanct and sometimes indistinguishable from the ideals that led to the formation of the institution. On the other hand, ideals don't exist in vacuums. They demand some degree of organization to become an effective force in our complex society. The drive for equal rights for Negroes, for instance, gave birth to the NAACP, to SNCC and CORE. Young people couldn't devote themselves to the needy in other lands without the help of organizations like the Peace Corps or the Papal Volunteers. Even love between a man and woman leads to the institution of marriage.

So what do you do with institutions? You can't live with them. You can't live without them.

As one wearied student expressed it over a cup of coffee: "I guess we need some kind of organization. I mean, I couldn't go to college unless the state or some people set it up and supported it. It's just that . . . well, you know: I never get the feeling that the people higher up care about *me*. They only want me to obey the laws. It's like a model railroad, and they're at the controls; it's a toy for them to fool around with. No one else has anything to say, like cogs in a machine."

What the troubled believer faces in the Church, he faces in all his future activities. He fears being swallowed up in a massive organization like General Motors where he'll be one among thousands of people. He knows it's going to happen, and he fears it. He wonders how he's going to preserve anything of himself when it happens. Will he become another faceless bureaucrat protecting his own self-interests, protecting his home in the suburbs, his new car and his children's education? The very anonymity of the system will make it easy for him to ride roughshod over the lives of others. He knows it, and he doesn't like it.

So what will he do? First he could turn off the switch in his mind and pretend that everything is just perfect. It's much easier to get along that way. He can join the Knights of Columbus, compliment Father after a pointless sermon and become a guiding light of the Holy Name Society. Or he could join the "system" out of necessity, without giving it his full allegiance; he'd always hold something back because he's lost hope that the system can change. Or finally he could reject the system or the organization completely.

And although it's pretty hard in our society to ignore General Motors, it's much easier to turn your back on the Church.

The trouble with these three possibilities is that they all reflect some degree of hopelessness and despair. They seem to say: "Things will never be different, so forget it. Give up now before the machine runs over you and destroys you. Take care of yourself, and let the system take care of itself." Eventually the onetime idealist retreats into isolation, because any reaction aimed at organizations as such leaves him to act on his own. And he runs the risk of amputating himself from the body of believers who laboriously preserved his own ideals through centuries of time.

The key word in all this is "hope." Not a hope that

minimizes present difficulties or pretends they don't exist. Not even a hope that looks forward to the day when this worldly Church will finally be perfect. That's like falling into a hole you just climbed out of. But young believers have reason to hope that they can find and help build a Church where they can be real persons, where they can speak and be listened to, where the system of doing things doesn't take precedence over the goals to be won. In the meantime, they can hope even though alienated from many aspects of the institutional Church today.

It's difficult for some older Catholics to understand this alienation of the younger believer from the Church as institution. It's hard for them not to attribute it to ingratitude and disrespect for authority. They have seen the Church rise from a beleaguered minority in the United States to a position of tremendous influence and power. They feel intense loyalty and pride in the institution through which vicariously they have made their way into prominence in American life.

The troubled young believer sees things differently. He has never known Catholicism which was not strong and powerful. The survival of an institution which can build multi-million-dollar schools and hospitals to rival those of the government is something he takes for granted. But he has a different priority. For him the problem is not survival but sincerity. He wants to learn how to keep his ideals and live in the suburbs too. Instinctively he turns to the Church as his source of ideals, for help and assistance.

What he hopes to find is that the Church will show itself to be more than an institution. He wants a community that is aware of his needs and wants to respond to them, not a giant that will run roughshod over him even as it purports to help.

This requires some institutional changes. Attempts have to be made to structure a lived and vital Christian community life where young people, together with older lay people, priests and nuns alike, can learn to work out together what being a Christian means in today's world. The troubled believer must come to believe that being a Catholic means more than holding on to what he has received. He must become convinced that following his own conscience as illuminated and influenced by the teaching Church is a valid and important way of being a Catholic.

Many Catholics, let it be admitted, don't rest easily with this kind of attitude. They sniff subjectivism in the air. But the world in which the troubled believer is being formed puts the highest premium on developing his own judgment and in having the honesty and courage to follow it. He is resentful of anyone who ignores or derides what he is trying to do. It is not arrogance or conceit, nor is it a question of his believing that he has the last word or the final truth. He is willing to listen but only if his advisors are. He accepts advice and correction only from those who show that they believe that what he has is probably good and may even be great. In a Church which believes that the Holy Spirit lives in each of its members, this shouldn't be too much to ask.

For a long time Catholics have met this particular problem — belief in an imperfect, highly organized, bureaucratic Church — by distinguishing between its divine and human elements. The Church is divine insofar as it preaches and protects the Gospel and communicates grace through the sacraments. All else is human and open to imperfection.

But grasping even this oversimplified response doesn't meet the particular problem of today's troubled believers. Their problem is rooted in a desire for a renewed vision of the Church's divinity. Other generations found this sense by tracing the Church back to Christ and the apostles, by proving that the sacraments were instituted by Christ and passed on by the apostles. Today's believers need something more. For them the divine — God — is seen in people not syllogisms. They are looking for a kind of loving concern and mutual respect for people which they and their culture have come to believe is the sign of God's presence and grace.

What they seek is not really radical or revolutionary. The Church, in fact, has already taken responsive steps. The American bishops have authorized adaptations in music for the liturgy of young people. Changes in the conduct of retreats with heavy emphasis on community and concern in liturgical worship and discussion have already given many young Catholics a new sense of their Church as their family.

To many it will seem that there is an unhealthy emphasis in many of the new adaptations on emotion and subjective experience. To deny this danger would be folly. But being paralyzed by it into an overly rational apologetics and preaching would be disaster. A Church in which most members believe because of reason and argument has never existed except in the pages of theology textbooks. In former cultures and times, the Church communicated God's presence in harvest prayers, local saints, in relics and rosaries. It was this sense of God's presence in the facts of local culture that produced faith, and so it must be today.

One of those facts today is the desire of young people to see institutions and organizations capable of spirit and life, capable of being, in other words, both human and divine. The way in which the Church responds to this challenge will determine to what extent it will hold the faith and deepen the faith of many of today's most sensitive, but troubled believers.

8 Where the Action Is

THEY are among the brightest and the most sensitive, and their problem with faith can't be wrapped neatly into psychological, moral or cultural categories.

For these it's the discovery that *religion and the Church just aren't where the action is.*

They may spell it out differently but the experience is pretty much the same.

The physics major puts it this way: "The laboratory excites me, and religion doesn't. When I'm in the lab or at my desk the hours disappear. When I get married I'll go to church with my wife, but it's going to be hypocritical. I don't disbelieve in God; it's just that the words have no meaning. I wish I could get excited about God and Mass and the sacraments but I can't. I've got my own world where things make sense, where things are real."

The fine-arts major came by a more gradual route. She used to visit a chaplain regularly to discuss questions of faith, but that was a couple of years ago.

"Those things don't bother me anymore. It's not that I've solved them. I guess I just ignore them. I get the feeling from the people I know that intelligent and sophisticated people don't bother about that sort of thing."

Others are even more blunt. "I just can't stand going to Mass anymore. It hit me one Sunday that I heard more important things about world problems from my sociology professor than I ever heard from that pulpit. I just can't stand hearing them repeat those same old platitudes when I know the world is going to hell."

They find themselves involved in the great question of the sacred and the secular, and by any other name it's just as thorny, just as complex.

Maybe there is still someone around who will try to get by with some quick phrases such as: "You're too materialistic . . . Unbelievers are immoral or corrupt . . . The Church is not just another social action agency." But the first time he tries it on one of these troubled believers will be his last chance with that person.

It may help to be told some things such as: "Belief in God is compatible with intense concern about his creation . . . Faith isn't primarily emotional . . . Many intelligent and sophisticated people *are* God-centered . . . The Church in many ways has gotten into the thick of civil rights." All these things are true, but it may not help to be told them right now.

The question is bigger than any of the easy answers.

Many young people have discovered meaning, purpose, morality and commitment outside a religious context. They have experienced a severe, if largely un-conscious emotional shock. They had been taught to look to prayer and the sacraments for the emotional sense of being joined to ultimate reality. They were taught to look to the saints for models, and to the commandments for morality and directions. In many instances they found what they were looking for when they were younger. But after discovering similar emotions and reactions in research, or creating a painting, in a professor or a non-believing friend, their religion can never be the same.

They have joined an increasing number of Catholics who have discovered the exciting possibilities of new worlds: research, artistic creation, social action. They have gotten involved, deeply involved or seen the possibility of doing so. And suddenly the absolute, ultimate claims of religion become a problem.

This isn't an intellectual problem. It's not a theoretical problem of whether belief in God is compatible with scientific research, or moral limitations on the activity of the artist. It's the discovery of the heady, intoxicating power of the secular world.

It used to be called secularism. Many still use the label. But it's a label that doesn't fit when you look at the whole picture. For secularism is a process which not only pushes God off the scene, but builds defenses against his coming back in. Secularism is a counter philosophy to religion. The secularist holds that life and its events contain within themselves all they need for their meaning.

The experience of these young believers, however, doesn't rule out religion or find God a threat. Frequently, in fact, it's accompanied by a nostalgia for the kind of satisfaction that religion used to bring and a wish that it could be that way again. The point is that something important, real and absorbing has been discovered. Religion, if it is to have any impact, must be able to produce the same kind of experience, only more so, since it claims to be superior, ultimate, the best.

The process might be called "secularization." There is no construction of a new self-contained religionless system. Rather we find things that used to be under religion's complete direction and guidance making their own peculiar demands. There was a time, for example, when religion and artistic experience were closely entwined. Paintings, music, sculpture were rooted in religious themes; they spoke directly of God, heaven and eternity as well as beauty, form and ecstasy. For the modern man this has all changed. Art speaks without reference to, or direction from above. So too with many other human experiences — politics, research, sexual love. For an increasing number of people these things produce experiences worth looking for and in some cases worth dying for because of their own value, and not because the Church says they are good or because they are good means of gaining eternal life.

These experiences of humanly valuable things don't shut out religion or make it useless, but they do set the terms on which religion becomes acceptable. The Church says it has something more, something better, something higher. Fine. But it will have to make itself felt in ways they know from experience are real and compelling. They think that they have discovered something of what beauty is, what spirituality is, what love and dedication are. They know these things are fragile and hard to keep. So if the Church wants to retain their allegiance it must not only match these deeply felt realities but do so in a depth or degree young people have not been able to find for themselves.

It is not either/or; it is competitive.

Religion, however, and especially Catholicism doesn't always like this kind of competition. For if there is a tendency on the part of the secularist to say: "This is practical; religion has no place here," there is a matching tendency on the part of religion. Some religious men have wanted to fence off an area called "grace" or the "supernatural" where the sacraments work and prayers are said and the only place it is expected to show is on some heavenly scoreboard.

It's convenient this way. On the one side you've got the world: politics, art, research, science, humanism. On the other is the Church: spiritual, supernatural, other-worldly, peaceful. To the man caught in the middle it's easy to believe that the Church is interested only in sex and stealing, things that might be mortal sins and thereby have a serious effect in the next life. This permits someone to think that he can play it "cool" and live pretty comfortably in two different worlds. Even allowing a few demerits for youthful indiscretions, he could end up a Knight of St. Gregory or some other version of the distinguished Catholic layman. This way everybody's happy; nobody's mad. The Church is the best (it says in the book) but it doesn't really have to show its hand until the next world. The world is second best (says the same book) but it can take responsibility for the real things — civil rights, housing, war and peace, art, the university.

It's in this kind of split-level existence that a typical young Catholic has been raised. He may have known within the Church deep and real spiritual experiences, possibly the most personal and important things he has ever known. But they bore little relationship to what has gone on in the rest of his world.

Then suddenly, one day, for some at least, that practical, everyday world comes vibrantly alive and begins to produce within him the kind of satisfactions he once knew in religion. It may be the song of a symphony, the hurt of a civil rights march, the dazzle of a Pollack, the comfort of a woman. Whatever it is, it's real, alive and it's — he knows there's a word for it — it's *spiritual*.

"Spiritual, religious, moral," the churchy words, are the only ones that fit this new reality, the feeling of having been awakened, of being part of something better and greater than himself. This is how religion is supposed to make him feel, but the experience is coming from that other place, the world, from things that have nothing apparently to do with religion and which in some cases seem opposed to it, or at least to its laws.

He finds himself taking the Church's power, the Church's words, the Church's authority and giving them to Albert Camus, Bob Dylan, J. D. Salinger, or painting, or friendship, or civil rights or even science. Increasingly he may sound like a secularist and act like a humanist, but inside he feels religious, like a Christian should, and the Church has got a fight on its hands to reclaim its special territory of religion.

Nature has made its stand, the nature we used to say grace could build on. It's probably better to say that grace presents itself "in nature" or "through nature." For the only grace that is real to most men is something that makes itself felt in the "life" they have discovered for themselves. If the Church is to make sense it will be in terms of life as it is now experienced and treasured.

The Christian faith has, in fact, the capacity to reach men at precisely this level and in exactly this way. For a troubled Catholic of the twentieth century to see God's saving hand and presence in a folk song or a humanist is essentially no different from earlier generations of Christians seeing that presence in pagan philosophers or pagan religious feast days. It's not easy. And it can't begin until Catholics learn to rest more easily with the turbulent, upset, changing, fragmented times in which they live.

This presumes of course that there should be some meeting of the sacred and secular. It presumes that locking each into its own airtight compartments is a bad thing. It presumes, too, that avoiding the issue and trying to pretend there is no struggle is also a bad thing.

But not everyone would agree, not everyone by a long shot.

Some Catholics don't want the Church to be "where the action is." To them places of action are places of confusion and uncertainty. They see the Church as primarily a place of refuge and calm. And these folks aren't all over thirty either.

The following incident expresses the viewpoint well. A young computer scientist was addressing a group of clergy interested in learning the new directions of science. After describing the exhilarating thrill of research and the excitement it produced in him, he added a footnote.

"I don't know," he said, "why you are here today, but this much I want you to know. I value my religion very highly for the contrast it affords to my hectic work. In the peace and calm of prayer and meditation I find a healthy antidote to the feverish pace that marks my working day."

Here is a man who is very happy that the Church isn't found where the action is. He has solved his conflict by making sure that the cares and concerns of the world don't have a chance to enter the sanctuary.

The point here is not who is right, the man who finds God in peace and quiet, or the man who finds him in the midst of human problems. And to say that there should be some of both doesn't help much either.

The point is that there is room in the Church for the troubled believers with their eager affirmation of the sacred in the secular. In fact it would seem that the spirit of aggiornamento released by Pope John and Vatican II require that room be made.

In *Pacem in Terris,* Pope John lamented the fact that Christianity had had and continues to have little effect on the great revolutionary events of our time. In *Mater and Magistra* and the council he began, you can see the same concern. In the ferment he created one can see a series of attempts to get the Church ready to begin to shape the technological, freedom-seeking, dignity-conscious world of our times.

To become that kind of influence the Church must have physicists who tell us how to conceive of God in an Einsteinian universe where stability is an illusion and process or change is the deepest reality. It needs artists who can show us how to see beauty and spirit in a world where nature exists only in game preserves and the whole world becomes a kind of plastic bubble. To be a shaping force in the world of revolution and change, the Church must have members who thirst for social justice with all the passion of a contemplative seeking God.

There is no guarantee that the Church has these kinds of members, or enough of them. Nor is there a demand that every Catholic be one.

But if the Church is going to be able to discern the moving presence of the Holy Spirit in the troubled waters of modern culture, it is going to be through the eyes of men who know how to navigate there, people who feel at home in the turbulence of change and ferment that many good people have for so long called materialism and secularism.

There is a new world being born today. It's where the action is. If the Church is ever going to influence it, it will probably be because its troubled believers stayed to help.

9 For Every Cloud

MAYBE not for every cloud, but for many of them when you are a Catholic in the late 60's, there's a silver lining. But for "silver lining" don't read miracle, quick-neat answer, free ride or trouble-free days are here again. That's just begging for more clouds, behind which silver linings may be harder to find.

You would have to be completely blind, and totally insensitive, however, not to have noticed that some remarkable things have been happening in the ancient Catholic Church.

The rock of Peter may not be eroding but it surely looks different bathed in the light of the religious revolution of the last decade. Revolution, incidentally, despite its political overtones, is not too strong a word for what has been going on.

The council, Vatican II of course, is the focus of the change, but the council is far from the whole picture. Apart from its context, in fact, the council could be a pretty disappointing specter.

Remember the days just before the council opened. The easiest thing in town to find was a visiting, eminent Church figure who summoned up all sorts of gloomy language in which to issue the warning: "Don't expect much. Nothing will happen."

Those were the days when talk of a vernacular liturgy was confined to a mimeographed bulletin which a few fringy people distributed, days when speakers at the National Liturgical Week were warned not to mention English in the Mass for fear of upsetting bishops, days when an eminent liturgical scholar was summarily blacklisted by a Catholic university because he favored the very things which a few years later the bishops approved.

Remember?

Those were the days when men like Yves Congar, Henri de Lubac, and John Courtney Murray were being told to be quiet about ideas and formulas for such things as religious freedom, that would within a short time find their way into documents approved by all the bishops, and who would on a given day find themselves concelebrating Mass with Pope Paul VI.

Remember?

Those were the days when the Catholic sky was peaceful all day, and nary a discouraging word was heard, when criticism was treasonous and the Church went before the world as a bastion of security in a changing world, and many could still believe that the Church was an attractive but almost lifeless heirloom of some more tranquil past.

Remember?

Those were the days when priests didn't go to

jail, and nuns didn't walk on picket lines, when a Protestant church was an enemy camp and an unbeliever a sinful renegade.

Remember?

It's not so long ago. Ten years ago.

This trek through memory is no parlor game, played for amusement. It's the touchstone of a revolution, an incredible change that no laws of history or sociology could predict or explain.

The evidence of the revolution may be the language in which we now offer our liturgy, the fasts that are no longer kept, the new cordiality between believers of a dozen professions. But these things are not the heart of the revolution. Their existence can be a hindrance to understanding what has really happened and what it says of the future, what it offers of hope to the troubled believer of today.

The troubled believer will take courage from aspects of the revolution in Catholicism that don't always make the headlines, from things that are not dramatically evident in his day-to-day life.

The first of these is the fact that nothing of importance occurred in the dramatic events of the council, or found its way into the carefully worded schemas, that had not been discussed, researched, written about and tested for at least thirty years before a council was even suggested. What the council did was to ratify, modify and formulate programs that had come from the grass roots of wherever men were thinking and praying about the future of religion. Without believers who were intensely aware of the movements of history, and the changing needs of men, and who were willing to break through thongs of tradition to make religion newly relevant, the council would have opened and almost certainly closed with nothing to draw upon but the tired phrases of theology manuals.

Now that might seem nothing more than an historical sidelight until you begin to realize that the council does not represent the last word to be spoken in human history on the subject of religion. There will have to be new generations with the courage of the old, to prepare for the theological breakthroughs of tomorrow. The troubled believer of today, who looks deep into his own questioning and just as deeply into his faith, and who tries with all his strength to build a bridge between the world he lives in and the faith he holds, is someone who in his own way, in his own time and place prepares for a council as yet uncalled, for a day not yet determined. Without many troubled believers to question the language of the liturgy, no change might have been made for generations yet to come.

A second fact about the Vatican Council which the troubled believer needs to recognize is that this was a council of *change,* not so much that it made changes, but that it identified the Church as in its very heart a organism which not only could change but of necessity must constantly change. Now this goes deep, and is a source of enormous pain for many Catholics who found in Catholicism a refuge, the one changeless thing in a constantly, frighteningly changing world. To "one, holy, catholic and apostolic," the council added another mark — "changing." What has been a source of pain, even trauma for some Catholics, should be for the young troubled believer a source of hope and courage.

The Church is not mired in some dusty past. It is taking steps in a dynamic present, responding to the same movements and forces which the young believer finds shaping and challenging his own belief. If the Church has not yet faced every question that troubles the young Catholic as squarely or successfully as he might want, he should remember that the council was not to be and cannot be the last word. It is simply an impetus and paradigm to believers to continue the search for the answers which are not yet expressed, and which we may never express as clearly as we might want. The council did more than make changes. It said clearly that the Church can expect to go on changing, that change is a sign of life.

This means that the council wasn't an end but a beginning.

And at this very moment, problems unmet by the council, problems that have come to the surface since it closed are being confronted by Christians everywhere in the spirit of reform, renewal and openess that was the mark of John XXIII.

Take the problems that confront the young and troubled believer: God, pluralism, the lure of the secular, the ambiguities of institutional religion. They trouble the Church as a community just as deeply as they affect the individual believer. The whole Church like the individual knows the pains of growing from age to age, of finding its identity in constantly changing historical and sociological patterns.

The point is that the Christian Church, in a slow and perhaps less dramatic manner, is going through the same crises of growth and questioning as the individual believer. Not only this, but it is coming up with some answers that should lead to exciting and challenging days for believers.

This is the age in which a pope can say: "Let the world know this: The Church looks at the world with profound understanding, with sincere admiration and with the sincere intention not of dominating it, but of serving it; not of despising it, but of appreciating it; not of condemning it, but of strengthening and saving it."

There is a revival of catechetics which hopefully will correct erroneous ideas about God so that "childish" ideas will be less of a problem in later life.

There are honest and sincere attempts to adapt the liturgy to the needs of men so they can pray in words and forms which mean something to them. The recent changes, hopefully, will be recognized as barely scratching the surface of the problem.

Christian thinkers are developing new and profound respect for the human person that is allowing breakthroughs in the fields of morality and religious practice.

There are council documents that, properly understood, dissipate the notion of a steamroller Church that seems blind and top-heavy. The notion of the Church as family takes its power not from the council declaring it so, but because it's a fact — God said it.

All Christians, not just clerics, are being seen deeply, perhaps for the first time, as bearers of God's life and truth. The Church is beginning to learn how to listen.

The Church is beginning to open up. Ecumenism

is destroying the myth that pluralism and religious convictions can't exist together.

There is more honesty in the Church, more encouragement of intellectual curiosity. The Index is gone. Popes talk to Marxists.

Anyone with a half hour to spare could list a dozen other manifestations of exciting movements within the Church.

But the problem is: exciting for whom?

The new movements contain within themselves the consummation of dreams harbored for many years by Catholic Christians and others. They hold the seed of an answer to dozens of questions. Father Andrew Greeley, for example, says: ". . . Those who are concerned can resolve their problems more readily today than they could twenty years ago. I think there is a good deal of evidence that the graduate student who has problems now can find people and books and. things in the changing Church that are much more helpful, than could a graduate student of twenty years ago."

But you have to believe in the Church as Church, you have to have an institutional commitment, before you really care or get excited about what happens in that institution.

Father James McGlynn, dean of the graduate school of the University of Detroit, puts it this way: "The generation now in its thirties and forties was, I suppose, able to accept the Church as an institution and then deepen their faith, whereas for many of today's bright young Catholics it seems that the deepening of faith must come first . . . We must therefore insist first on Christ and our union with him, and only then on the

Church as an institution. We must present the Church through Christ rather than Christ through the Church."

This is probably why the radically exciting movements which converged in the council, and which have sprung from its documents don't draw the kind of response from students that their teachers think they should. Some college students were asked: "What do you think of the council?" The replies came out like this: "Not much really . . . They never really got around to the things that were troubling me . . . Pope John really got me excited, but the council. Well! . . . Gee, it does look like the Church might do something."

Youngsters are impatient and naturally simplistic. They are at a period of their life when they easily discard anything and everything which doesn't register an immediate impact. If it means something to me personally, it stays; otherwise out it goes. There is little room for complexity or depth. And it works for a while. The problem is that very soon the things which mean much to the youngster lose their impact, and the complexities, the things which can sustain belief, are abandoned.

Right now there are important and faith-sustaining movements of progress and development within and without the Church. In these movements, in these fresh ideas are responses to the questions most felt by the young troubled believer, and at least partial answers and partial solutions to their questionings.

But at the moment many of these youngsters can't see the brighter future. They can't really appreciate the answers because they have not yet come to that point where it matters that much to them what the Church does, if anything.

Right now the question is as basic as God.

It's a question of faith.

10 Ask Abraham

THERE were perhaps fifteen of us around the plastic-topped cafeteria tables eating chips, drinking coffee and discussing religion. There were students, young marrieds, a couple of doctors, a lawyer, some middle-aged parents. And the question on the floor was faith.

The believers were asking: "What is faith?"

"It's believing something," said one, "without being able to prove it."

"For me," said another, "it's more intellectual than emotional."

A third dredged up a catechism answer: "It's the assent of the mind to something God has said."

At some point someone mentioned Christ. "It's my response to Christ and to other people."

Then there was silence, until someone said quietly. "That's not much to go on, is it?"

And everyone agreed with shaking heads that indeed it wasn't much to go on in a world of nuclear physics, moon shots and cultural revolution.

So, what is faith? What is enough?

Ask Abraham. He was the first of the believers, the father of our faith. Here is a man who experiences God in ways that are neither clear nor important, but surely enough and strongly enough to make him leave his own land, journey to another and enter into an alliance with one supreme God. However it happened one thing is clear: God made the advance to Abraham. He chose this man out of thousands for reasons hidden in God's own being, and selected him to begin a mission by which this God would be made known to all men of all times. The election of this one man is followed by promises: a nation will emerge from his loins, in time his descendants will have their own land, and all men will be in some way blessed because of Abraham. The key promise must have seemed preposterous: Abraham and his wife were old and long since without hope of children. Yet strange as the promises must have seemed, Abraham enters into the treaty, the covenant proposed by this God who approached him. He believes in him.

The key promise is kept. A son is born to Abraham and his wife, only to have God make the incredible command that the boy should be killed as a sacrifice. And still Abraham believes in his God. Only at the last moment, when God again appears, is the execution prevented.

In a way the details are not important, but the total picture is. In Abraham's belief in God the pattern of all belief is established.

God takes the initiative in belief. He makes the

advance. He speaks when and where he pleases and to whom he chooses.

It's personal. God comes to a man with an invitation to enter into a personal relationship, not just to accept a disembodied doctrine.

Experience of God has the aspect of a "mission." It may begin within the individual, but its end is always the family of man. God aligns himself with some men only that all others might also see and believe.

The experience can and often does and radically should change the entire pattern of a man's life. In Abraham's case the external signs of change were dramatic (a new home and an unexpected fatherhood), but the interior demands can be every bit as strong.

Faith is that confidence in another, in God, which is so certain that a man does not hesitate to hand his whole life over into the keeping of the one in whom he believes.

Ask Abraham and this is what he will tell you.

Ask Moses and he too will have an answer.

Like Abraham he finds himself selected seemingly at random. He is to give birth not to a son but to a nation. In him promises made to Abraham will be kept. The invitation is personal but the consequences will affect all men. A huddled band of slaves will be led out of captivity into freedom, and out of their diversity God is to shape a people who will have as their only common ground faith in the God who has freed them.

Faith becomes a saving thing. Once they were slaves, now they are free. The strong arms of God have held back their oppressors and led them toward a land of promise.

Faith is a community experience. Believers can't stand alone. They are joined by a common experience into a chosen people, who together must keep alive the covenant that God has made with men. They have become brothers by means of a common father.

Faith brings responsibility. The God experienced is a lawgiver who insists that those who are to be numbered among his people must live in ways that will demonstrate his own holiness and fidelity.

Faith can be fickle. Men have short memories and they soon forget their former slavery and him who makes them free. They are easily attracted by other gods and other promises.

But the God of faith is true. He keeps his word. Nothing can dissuade him from the promises he made. He awaits, in patience, the return of his people when they have strayed.

He is also a God of history. He reveals himself in the events of time. In the deeds of kings, in the movements of liberators, in time and in space he makes himself known, who he is and what he desires.

The God of faith is above all else beyond the imaginings of men. "No one can look upon my face and live." He will not be reduced to words or formulas, to here and not there, to this image or to that description. He is simply he who is, he who is with man, not visible, not overpowering man or substituting for him, but simply present to man.

Ask Moses what faith is and this is what he will tell you of his own.

Speak also to the prophets — to Amos, Osee, Isaias

and Jeremias — to those believers whose mission was to recall Israel to belief.

Speak to Amos, the rough-hewn shepherd, whose name means "strong," and listen to what he has seen of God. He is a prophet of justice who cast his denunciations before the faces of the mighty.

The God of Amos' faith is a just God who will not tolerate injustice among those to whom he has given his word. Oppressors of the poor, wielders of power, will feel his sting.

Believers must be worthy of the call, the care, the love of him who offered his friendship.

Faith is not taking God for granted, for although its end is in peace and joy, the journey must often be made in caution and fear.

Speak to Osee who knew the love of God for his people. Let him tell you of how at the instruction of God he married a harlot whom he cherished and welcomed back even after she had been unfaithful to him.

Faith is a marriage between God and man. It is a bond of love. God is the eternal lover and man his unfaithful spouse. But as often as man shall fail, he will be welcomed back into the love of God. God has joined man and himself together. He desires that no act of man put asunder the union.

Faith is the bond of a Father and son. "When Israel was a child I loved him; out of Egypt I called my son. The more I called them, the farther they went from me, sacrificing to the Baals and burning incense to idols. Yet it was I who taught Ephraim to walk, who took them in my arms: I drew them with human cords, with bands of love: I fostered them like one who raises an infant to his cheeks; yet though I stopped to feed my child, they did not know that I was their healer." (Osee 11, 1-4)

Speak to Isaias, who through the reigns of three kings was a prophet of the holiness of God, who called men to a faith marked by adoration and contemplation of their God.

God is a holy God, his glory a light that the eyes of men cannot endure. He is the Lord, King, the Strong One, the Powerful One.

Faith is an absolute. Complete confidence is its mark. Total comitment to the Lord is required.

Speak also to Jeremias, a man who accused God of having sent him on a fool's errand.

Faith is a foolish man, a laughingstock who knows that in his foolishness "a strength greater than mine overmastered me."

Faith is to be known by God in the depths of your heart, to be called by your own name.

Faith is to know that there are no temples built by man which cannot be destroyed.

Faith knows no earthly reward.

Faith is not the law.

So what is faith? What is enough?

Faith is Abraham, Moses, Amos, Osee, Isaias, Jeremias and a hundred others, shepherds and kings, peasants and prophets.

Faith is an advance from a God who is free in his choice, a savior, a maker of peoples, true to his promises, a shaper of history, beyond man's grasp, just, a protector of the poor, a lover of his spouse, a father to unfaithful sons, holy, a caller of men's names, a searcher of their hearts.

Faith is an invitation accepted, a mission received, membership in a people of choice, life turned in its tracks, freedom, responsibility, obedience to law, an experience of failure, an end to being alone, a judgment, fear, a marriage, sonship, prayer, adoration, commitment, total gift, foolishness.

Faith is fear and trembling.

Faith is the terror of falling into the hands of the living God.

Faith is certainty but not security.

Faith is love.

Faith is Jesus Christ.

For in Jesus Christ the God of Abraham, Isaac and Jacob is made visible, and the response of Abraham, Isaac and Jacob is made perfect.

In the unity of a single person, Christ is God inviting and man responding.

He is God. The same God whose voice Abraham somehow heard, but now with a Nazarean accent. The same God whose face Moses once begged to see, but was forbidden at the cost of death, now has a face that can burn in a summer sun, crease with tears, and relax in repose. This is God, the same God whose call, whose claim is heard by generation after generation from behind the appearances of the world he made. This is the God whom one man glimpses in a sunrise, another in a work of art, another in a scientific truth, through the needs of all men or in the face of someone he loves. This is the claim, the invitation, the advance made personal, substantial, tangible.

He is also man: the only man who in himself offered an adequate response to the invitation of God. He is what the believer yearns to be, perfect in his acceptance of God's claim on his love, faithful through every temptation.

In him man finds a model of what it means to believe.

In him man finds God speaking, demanding.

A believer, like Christ, is a man about his father's business. He is a man of empathy and compassion for the sinner, for the sick, the imprisoned, the starving and the bereaved. He is a tempted man, and a man of prayer. He is a witness and a prophet. He knows sorrow and misunderstanding. He can expect suffering and death. But he can look forward to a resurrection.

Christ is, however, more than a model for believers.

It is through and with and in Christ that men believe. Joined to Christ a man can do what he could never do by himself: make an adequate response to God.

The union of Christ and man is not poetic imagining, but it takes poetry to grasp it.

Christ is a vine and men are the branches.

Christ is the head and men are the body.

A Christian believes not just because of Christ but in Christ. He not only discovers God but responds to God in Christ.

So what is faith? What is enough?

The Christian says that his faith is Christ.

He says that Christ alone is enough.

Without Christ a man might find his experience of God too distant, too vague. And without Christ a man might despair when he compared the claims of the God he has experienced with the fragility of his own response.

But with Christ, in Christ and through Christ weakness becomes strength, gestures however inadequate become enough.

11 The Way It Is

IN THE student-filled ballroom of the convention hotel the brilliant and well-known Catholic layman finished his talk and asked for questions.

"Will you tell us please," asked the young woman, "why you are still a Catholic?"

There was hardly a pause before he answered:

"Lord to whom shall we go?" He elaborated, but that was the heart of it.

A few hours later an equally well-known priest-theologian faced the same audience and heard the same question.

The pause was longer, much longer before the answer came.

"Because," he said in essence, "of the resurrection."

But this time the young lady was not to be put off. "That explains why you're a Christian," she answered, "but why are you a Catholic?"

"Because of the eucharist," was the somewhat abashed reply.

On the sidelines were a hundred or so college chaplains, at least some of them quietly grateful that they hadn't been put on the same spot. You were one of the grateful ones; grateful that, at least, the question didn't come so publicly to you. But at the same time you knew it had to be answered because deep inside it was demanding an answer.

You remembered too the insight of another chaplain: "When a kid comes by the office and tells you he doesn't believe in God, he isn't asking you for reasons why he should. He's asking why *you* do."

So it wasn't as though you could avoid the question even if you wanted to. It's like being at the side of Christ when he asked: "What do you think of the Son of Man?" There was and is no ducking an answer.

But what constitutes an answer?

Two plus two equals four. But what is faith the sum of?

There is a temptation to reach back in memory and run through the whole apologetical argument that centuries of scholars have knit together. In its web of history, philosophy, scripture and common sense there is more than enough evidence for assuring that your act of faith is a reasonable thing. It comes in handy on the day when the whole business of believing seems little more than an acceptable form of madness. But it doesn't say much about your faith, how it came to be, why you cling to it, what it means to you.

Nobody, on the other hand, is asking for a biography. It's probably true that without Catholic parents, schools and influences you might at this moment be explaining why you are still an atheist, a humanist, or some other kind of religious man. But the sum of names, dates and places is a framework not an answer.

You're not Abraham and there have been no divine commands that changed your name and home and gave you a son for a sign. You're not Moses and you've never seen a burning bush and led slaves out of captivity and heard the voice of God on a mountain top.

But you believe what they believed. Maybe not so well. But you do believe, so there must be something. And there is. It isn't exact and brilliantly clear, but some things you have learned about faith, your faith, things which you learned not from books or teachers but by keeping your eyes open, watching others, watching yourself, trying day by day, or, at least, from time to time, to live like a man who believes.

And when you've said that much you've already said that you learn the hard way.

It is hard, for example, to learn to live with a faith that isn't perfect. Books and teachers inevitably talk about faith, and for that matter all of the other virtues, in terms of the ideal. They leave the impression that the only real faith is perfect faith. As a result you begin to wonder whether a faith as troubled as yours sometimes is, as up-and-down as it is, is really faith at all.

It takes time to realize that in every believer there is a strain of unbelief, that most of us are not really "believers" but sinful men in the process of becoming believers. Perfection is not the only standard of sincerity and true faith.

Part of the same package is learning that you have to be yourself and not someone else. That's the sort of advice that you hear from the time you are a small child, but rarely does it get applied to the matter of religion. It's not a case of finding a model for yourself and deciding that this or that person is a "real" Catholic and that's what you've got to be like. This path leads straight to frustration. Either you're going to end up a pious phony or an ex-Christian. You can't be St. Panathagoras, or your cousin the monk, or that awfully "nice chap" that lives across the street. You've got to be yourself, the kind of Christian you can be and not somebody else's ideal.

And here we are at the heart of *real, actual* belief. Accepting God and accepting yourself, believing in God and yourself, are two sides of the same coin. It's a lot easier said than done. Father Walter Gouch, the wise, veteran chaplain at John Hopkins University says: "To ask for perfect identification at any level before death is almost meaningless, and when we ask for perfection before death, to a large extent we are treating man as a rational animal, forgetting he is this only by definition. All that he actually is, is a possibility of reason, a possibility of freedom and a possibility of love." This means from our point of reference that perfect faith in God — which means perfect identification with self — is just out of the question during most lifetimes. "For the divine is part of the total reality," he adds, "with which you can begin to identify only if you start with yourself, and can accept yourself." In pointed, pedestrian terms, therefore, if you have a false or phony image of yourself you are going to end up with a faith that is false and phony.

Another way of saying the same thing is this: getting to that faith described in sermons is going to take a lifetime, and it's going to be a painful process. So in the meantime don't cut yourself down for not being perfect.

From this another fact about real faith should be obvious.

Faith isn't a blank check on happiness. No one ever said that if you believe the pain of being a human being is just going to disappear. Faith isn't a back door out of the human condition. Faith doesn't change the facts of life, it just lets you see them in a different light. It lets you see into them and through them. Pains don't hurt less because you know there is a God; it's just that in their midst you know that they aren't the whole story.

Faith isn't a nothing-now-everything-later proposition, the one that used to be called "Pie in the sky when you die." It isn't to chicken out on life so that to the starving man, or the enslaved man, or the naked man you can say "It'll all be all right in the next world." It doesn't permit handing out pious goodies to a man who needs food. Faith is saying "yes" to God, but the "yes" is said here and now, where the needs are, where the claims are made, where the questions are asked, where God makes himself felt, where love is challenged.

Faith isn't a crutch or a set of blindfolds. It isn't the refuge of cowards. It isn't, in Sister Jacqueline's phrase "a measure of caution," but rather "a measure of new power." From faith, she said, "should come a sense of power that would enable us to live in tension, that would allow us, at times, to live in torment." A man of faith is not one who ignores the conditions of life, but sees in their absurdities and impossibilities the raw material of a living faith, a faith which exercises itself in service far beyond that point where a man might understandably quit in despair.

Faith is many things and few of them are easy or automatic.

Faith is seeing God in your own world just as surely as Abraham and Moses saw him in theirs. And what makes us think he was easier to see than he is now?

If there is a God he is as visible in New York and Santa Fe as he was in Chaldea and Egypt. Here and now there are promises to be heard, children of faith to be born, bushes that burn and slaves to be freed.

It is a question of recognizing them.

In the midst of heat spells and droughts, in air-conditioned offices and crowded expressways, in open fields and mazes of concrete, in classrooms and bedrooms, in glowing faces and broken bodies, on assembly lines and food lines there is a voice to be heard and a face to be seen.

On the mountain road in Vermont when the sun had set and a damp breeze had begun to move down the hillsides and across the fields, God could be known. He was there in the sudden knowledge of infinite desires and finite realities. To know that in a man's heart there is no end to dreaming, and in his soul no end to thirst, was to hear God's voice.

On the lined face and in the crippled limbs of the

woman whose body had known through decades a hundred pains, and whose hopes had known a hundred defeats but whose generosity had never faltered and whose love was the best she could do, was to know God.

In the bent shoulders and the tired eyes of the man who had never known a moment of acclaim and to whom success had never come, but who had been faithful to his promises and who had never asked for anything for himself, was also to know God.

In the faces of a hundred youngsters on that hot, South Carolina afternoon with that curious mingling of fear and courage, in their linked arms and strong voices as they faced arrest and imprisonment and shame and things they could't guess for the sake of a thousand others whose color had enslaved them, the voice of God was clear.

In the haunted eyes of the young boy who wanted to love but who didn't know how, and whose memories had brought him to the bank of a river and the edge of death, the face of God could be seen.

In the softened features and failing voice of the woman who for forty years fed the poor and fought for justice, and who had never known or cared about how to meet tomorrow, God was present.

In the joy of the young teacher who spent her days among "retarded" children who would never grow and for whom kindness was a miracle, he was present.

Here are the burning bushes, the slaves to be freed.

For God is where he walks, where his voice can be heard, where the features of his face can be traced.

He is where love is or in its absence cries to be.

The young girl said: "When I doubted life, then I

doubted God. But that's a difficult thing to do, to doubt life."

When you do doubt life, when you do doubt love, you must doubt God. It doesn't follow that everyone who affirms life will affirm God, but no one who does not affirm life and love can ever affirm God.

For faith is saying yes to reality, not just in its appearances but at its heart. It is to find in a sunset, a mountain peak, the curiosity of a child, the courtesy of age, the pain of disappointment, the loss of death, in all things a call to love and be loved.

It is to find at the heart of the universe a person, and to find that love is the meaning of the universe.

Once seen, once responded to, faith is not easily lost. But this does not mean that the man of faith is destined to live his days in a world bathed in splendor.

There will inevitably be, again in the phrase of Sister Jacqueline, "periods of terrible darkness and terrible unknowing." There will be days when the vision will become clouded or seem to disappear altogether. Days when the surface of reality will refuse to give way to its inner meaning. Days when the thought of God will seem like a mad hoax and love a terrifying sham.

There will be days that bring neither joy nor comfort.

On those days there will be nothing to do but to hold on with naked conviction to the vision once seen clearly and surely in a hundred different faces of the world.

On these days it will be necessary to pray in darkness as one who doubts to a God who does not make himself felt. It will be necessary to stand in the loneliness of one's faith without consolation and reward.

From these days should emerge a faith that is at once deeper and purer, in which the depth of one's certainty comes not from the attractiveness of the evidence but the character of the God whose love has been offered and received.

Faith. A curious thing. An absurdity to those who do not believe, a puzzle to those who do.

Faith. A free gift of a loving God. But a gift that is given subject to all the laws by which a man lives and grows. Beyond psychology, but knit into the fiber of a man's psychological growth. The same in all times and places but colored by every time and place.

Faith. The sturdiest of commitments, but as fragile as love.

And why do you still believe?

Who can really say why? Who can say more than in the face of reality, in experiences forgotten or only half-remembered, a voice was heard, a face was seen, a conviction grew, a reality was grasped beyond that which was seen.

The world had meaning. There was a claim on your love.

And "Lord to whom shall we go?"